ARCHITECTURAL DESIGN
Vol 69 No 3/4 March-April 1999

EDITORIAL OFFICES:
42 LEINSTER GARDENS, LONDON W2 3AN
TEL: + 44 171 262 5097 FAX: + 44 171 262 5093

EDITOR: Maggie Toy
EDITORIAL ASSISTANT: Bob Fear
PRODUCTION: Mariangela Palazzi-Williams
COPY EDITOR: Melissa Larner
DESIGN: Mario Bettella and Andrea Bettella/Artmedia
ADVERTISEMENT SALES: 01243 843272

CONSULTANTS: Catherine Cooke, Terry Farrell, Kenneth Frampton, Charles Jencks, Heinrich Klotz, Leon Krier, Robert Maxwell, Demetri Porphyrios, Kenneth Powell, Colin Rowe, Derek Walker

SUBSCRIPTION OFFICES:

UK: JOHN WILEY & SONS LTD
JOURNALS ADMINISTRATION DEPARTMENT
1 OAKLANDS WAY, BOGNOR REGIS
WEST SUSSEX, PO22 9SA, UK
TEL: 01243 843272 FAX: 01243 843232
E-mail: cs-journals@wiley.co.uk

USA AND CANADA:
JOHN WILEY & SONS, INC
JOURNALS ADMINISTRATION DEPARTMENT
605 THIRD AVENUE
NEW YORK, NY 10158
TEL: + 1 212 850 6645 FAX: + 1 212 850 6021
CABLE JONWILE TELEX: 12-7063
E-mail: subinfo@wiley.com

ANNUAL SUBSCRIPTION RATES 1999: UK £135.00 (institutional rate), £90.00 (personal rate); Outside UK US$225.00 (institutional rate), $145.00 (personal rate). AD is published six times a year. Prices are for six issues and include postage and handling charges. Periodicals postage paid at Jamaica, NY 11431. Air freight and mailing in the USA by Publications Expediting Services Inc, 200 Meacham Ave, Elmont, Long Island, NY 11003.

SINGLE ISSUES: UK £18.99; Outside UK $29.95. Order two or more titles and postage is free. For orders of one title please add £2.00/$5.00. To receive order by air please add £5.50/$10.00.

POSTMASTER: send address changes to AD, c/o Publications Expediting Services Inc, 200 Meacham Ave, Elmont, Long Island, NY 11003.

Printed in Italy. All prices are subject to change without notice.
[ISS N: 0003-8504]

CONTENTS

ARCHITECTURAL DESIGN **MAGAZINE**

ARCHITECTURAL DESIGN **PROFILE** NO 138

SCI-FI ARCHITECTURE

Peter Einsenmann, Center for the Arts, Emory University, Atlanta

Edible Architecture – Greek Street cake event

Coop Himmelb(l)au, Cloud # 9, Geneva

SHIFTING THE DISCIPLINE OF ARCHITECTURE
TRANSFORMATIONS IN ARCHITECTURAL EDUCATION AND PEDAGOGY
by Sharon Haar

Architectural education as we know it today began to take shape with the codification of societal power relationships during the late-18th century Enlightenment. This is expressed in Claude-Nicholas Ledoux's engraving of the auditorium of the Theatre of Besançon, reflected in the eye of the architect. Ledoux's image constructs a 'reciprocal relationship' between authority and society through a social contract in which authority is given over to leaders who are in turn responsible for reflecting society's will.[1] Traditional models of architectural practice exist in the space defined by this gaze, implying not only that the architect is capable of knowing and responding to the will of society, but additionally that what constitutes an appropriate response is carefully circumscribed. Similarly, the boundaries of architectural education exist within the limits of these reciprocally constructed cones of vision. They are codified in the legal control of the title 'architect', the desire to bring all schools under a single accreditation system, and the devaluation of the licence to practise architecture to an increasingly mechanised examination of the ability to protect 'health, safety, and welfare'.[2]

This reflective outlook directs recent proposals to make architectural education mirror architectural practice more closely. Such proposals decrease classroom and studio instruction to support an increase in 'co-operative' and 'practice-studio' experiences. Advocates of 'professionalisation' would dismantle the educational system that was built in the 19th century to legitimate the profession, in order to become more transparent to late-20th-century conditions, acknowledging the complex, global, and competitive qualities of architectural practice.[3] Thus, each year the required knowledge and responsibility of the architect expands, the demands put upon schools for accreditation become more sophisticated, and the requirements for licensing become more constrained. While these changes may be productive, they are a short-term fix for the expanded needs of practice in a fragmented, yet global, environment.

This defence of the territory of the profession is in part a reaction to the blurring of traditional disciplinary boundaries and a perceived decrease in the market share for traditional architectural services. As Donna Haraway states: 'The stakes in the border war have been the territories of production, reproduction, and imagination'. She argues for '... pleasure in the confusion of boundaries and for responsibility in their construction'.[4] Who can legitimately be described as an architect? What is the place of architecture, indeed what is architecture, within our new virtual, urban, and global environments? Are we to reduce the definition of architecture to 'buildings' or expand it to encompass new virtual and urban environments? Who defines what we teach as architecture?

Mapped onto architecture, Haraway's manifesto suggests that in the 21st century we will need to reconfigure the borders of architecture, not just defend them against assault. We will also need to diversify the structure of architectural education.

Disciplinary boundaries and the global environment of architecture

A discipline is defined by its contents, its boundaries, and the rules that regulate those boundaries. Specific perspectives order what a discipline contains and how it is delimited.[5] Neither the discipline of architecture nor its relationship to the profession is 'natural' or unchanging. Complex relationships among schools, the profession, and various regulatory agencies determine who may be called an architect and what practices are properly defined as architectural.

After developing into a specific set of design practices in 19th-century industrial societies, architectural firms of the mid-20th century came to be structured by hierarchical control and oversight. Large multidisciplinary companies tended to reinforce rather than redefine the divisions between design tasks. Through this process, standardised architectural products could be exported worldwide.[6] The explosion of information technologies and socio-economic restructuring in the late-20th century – the 'space of flows' – created a new environment for practice.[7] This has produced a great transformation of the environments within which, and for which, architects design. There has also been a restructuring of how and with whom architects practise. Finally, and most commonly acknowledged, flexible patterns of work and a focus on information gathering and processing[8] have transformed all scales of architectural practice.[9]

Recently, certain interdisciplinary practices have expanded or emerged that do not fall neatly within the traditional boundaries of the profession: community development and empowerment, public policy, planning and zoning, ecology and the environment, installation and artistic practices, curatorship, publishing and criticism, and preservation. The greatest opportunity may lie in the electronic/virtual environment with its potential to affect the shape and nature of physical environments. This is evident in the increasing number of practices concerned with the design of the virtual environment, including advanced rendering and animation, website design and interactive communication, and new forms of 'space-planning' involving the interaction of physical and virtual space. These practices recognise the virtual environment as more than a graphic realm, as a new form of space.

Contemporary feminist theory is useful for understanding these 'boundary practices' because their work and strategies are characteristic of the marginal spaces, identities, and existences traditionally inhabited by women. The feminisation of the professions is not just the result of women entering the workplace but also a transformation in the nature and product of the work itself. What some see as a profession 'out of control', others call a 'fear of the feminine', a permeable and unstable state: '... to sell himself in the global marketplace, the "old boy" must be fragmented, moulded and reconstructed as a "new girl"'.[10]

The permeability of boundaries in the global environment undermines the circumscribed power and social relationships described by Ledoux's image. Speaking of the status of the architectural object, Beatriz Colomina notes that 'this disturbance of boundaries has often been understood as a threat to identity, a loss of self".[11] The same is true of architectural practice: as its boundaries become more permeable, the profession's desire for control increases. This is clearly occurring in its increased self-regulation and in its attempts to regulate schools. However, the restructuring of architectural education must reflect the restructuring of late-20th-century practice.

New curricular challenges

Technologies and scientific discourses can be partially understood as formalisations, ie, as frozen moments, of the fluid social interactions constituting them, but they should also be viewed as instruments for enforcing meanings.[12]

A curriculum is an instrument for 'enforcing meanings'. Understood as a set of courses constituting an area of specialisation, the focus of a curriculum is on time, units, skills, data and sequences that codify quantifiable knowledge and abilities into structured relationships. From the Latin *currere* (to run), a curriculum is like a current: both of the moment and continuously moving. To conceive a curriculum in this manner is to recognise it as a structure that forms connections within the fluid condition that is our multicentred and fragmented environment. Although architectural education no longer consists of a discrete body of knowledge offering a unified paradigm in response to a civic or social claim, it can transform to teach students to engage in multiple and flexible forms of practice. Today's colleges and universities must fulfil two requirements: first, create critical thinkers who can interact within the power relations and social processes of rapid information exchange, and second, train workers for jobs in the global marketplace. Current structures of architectural education do not adequately address these potentially conflicting knowledge and skill requirements. Nonetheless, recent discussions about the structure of architectural education focus on an accounting of credit hours and the number of years required for a professional degree rather than addressing the need to restructure the goals and forms of this education.[13]

Typically, discussions of the relationship between the profession and the academy take the form of a jeremiad organised around a series of single-issue debates: the role of liberal arts education, degree designation, the battle between theory and practice, or the split between social and formal concerns in design. At the same time, numerous schools, conferences, and professional organisations have recognised the restructuring of architectural practice within the context of globalisation, the shift from hard to soft technologies, emerging economies, and urban and ecological degradation.[14] Although they now embrace new forms of practice, these groups often dismiss the need to consider new practices within the academy, instead calling for greater control over professional education.

While the 'gap' between the profession and the academy may be widening, the scope of concern still remains very narrow. There may be advantages to maintaining this distance.[15] bell hooks proposes that we celebrate rather than bridge this gap, recognising a new opportunity for practice. She writes:

> To some extent, ruptures, surfaces, contextuality, and a host of other happenings create gaps that make space for oppositional practices which no longer require intellectuals to be confined by narrow separate spheres with no meaningful connection to the world of the everyday.[16]

In order to allow for these shifts in practice we need to acknowledge the instability and impermeability of the discipline of architecture itself. And we must educate students not only to accommodate themselves to the vicissitudes ahead but also to become active agents in their own educational and career choices. Education should combine an understanding of physical space with knowledge of the processes that shape this space – allowing students to see these new processes not as negative challenges but as creative possibilities.

Architectural education in the 21st century

If architectural practices are becoming more interdisciplinary, and if increasing numbers of graduates are moving into fields not traditionally seen as architectural, how should architectural education respond? The following is an outline of one possible proposal, which suggests an offensive rather than defensive reaction to disciplinary change. It is premised on a clarification of professional education that situates this education predominantly within graduate programmes. This would create a space of opportunity within undergraduate programmes, which would become strictly 'pre-professional'. The proposal provides for a flexible structure that resolves a number of the conflicts described above.

Firstly, no longer focused on the singular pursuit of an architectural degree, undergraduate education should be open to a greater number of practices. Studio work should still remain at the core of this education because it is the problem-solving, process-oriented abilities and ways of thinking that can be extended to other disciplines and careers. Pre-professional programmes could then vary from school to school in response to the needs of local constituencies. What all programmes would share would be a concentration on the discipline of architecture, an enlarged liberal arts core, and an introduction to a broad array of post-graduate possibilities through an interdisciplinary 'professional practices' course and a 'co-op' opportunity for upper-level students. Equipped with a greater range of information about post-graduate opportunities, students can take greater responsibility for their education and career choices. Graduates will also enlarge the public understanding of the physical environment and the role of architecture in shaping it by bringing their architectural experience to bear on other careers.

Second, professional graduate programmes should be better equipped to become sites of research and global exchange. Students will enter such programmes more broadly educated in both the liberal arts and architecture. Standard 'professional practice' courses and studio projects could take on the more complex demands of the practice of architecture within a restructured global environment, engaging more diverse programmes, constituencies, and sites. Third, graduate programmes should continue to diversify. Specialised graduate programmes in digital design, for instance, are already in formation. These are better suited to students who want to work in the design of virtual rather than physical space. Other interdisciplinary graduate programmes are also possible under such a model. All graduate programmes should require extra-curricular practical experience as part of the educational programme, carefully tied to the research and professional concerns of each subject area.

Compelling contemporary educational structures to meet the complex demands of today's practices is simultaneously repressive and inadequate. Like the tools and technologies that we use to shape our environment, the curricular structure that we utilise to educate our students is not value-free. This proposal does not resolve all of the difficulties inherent in the restructured global environment of architecture. There is not space here to go into the detailed reworking of licensing, accreditation, and course content that such a proposal requires and which would be necessary for greater articulation between worldwide institutions.

An active engagement with new disciplines, technologies, communities, and environments is one route toward the diversification of the profession. As educators we have the opportunity and responsibility to reflect the cultural diversity of the communities from which we come and which we serve; to answer the questions: what is our context, who are our students, what do they want from their education, and what are we educating them for? Each institution will find different answers to these questions and build a curriculum around their answers. For even within a global environment, flexible and constantly restructuring, we are always engaged in a specific context. Education must mirror the multicentred and fragmented environments of contemporary practice and society and empower students with the knowledge, skills, and flexibility to design for them.

Sharon Haar is an architect and Director of the Bachelor of Arts in Architectural Studies programme at the University of Illinois, Chicago. This is an edited version of a paper presented in Rio de Janeiro, Brazil, in 1998, reprinted with permission of Constructing New Worlds: Proceedings of the 1998 ACSA International Conference, *published by the Association of Collegiate Schools of Architecture.*

Notes

1 '... the beam of light that illuminates the stage, emanating from the back of the auditorium, is also reflected in the pupil, but is then projected, like the all-seeing eye of Masonic iconography, from inside the orb itself out towards the spectator'. Anthony Vidler, *The Writing of the Walls*, Princeton Architectural Press (New York), 1987, p40.

2 This paper deals specifically with conditions in the United States, but as I will argue, the global conditions under which architecture is practised today make its claims pertinent to educational institutions and practices worldwide.

3 One of the strongest public attacks on the schools was Michael J Crosbie's, 'The Schools: How They're Failing the Profession (and What We Can Do About It)', *Progressive Architecture* 126, September 1995, pp47-51. Robert Gutman offers a more reasoned perspective in 'Two Discourses on Architectural Education', *Practices* 3/4, Spring 1995, pp11-19. See also, Robert Gutman, 'Redesigning Architecture Schools' *Architecture* 85, August 1996, pp87-89.

4 Donna Haraway, *Simians, Cyborgs, and Women: The Reinvention of Nature*, Routledge (New York),1991, p150.

5 Elizabeth Grosz, *Volatile Bodies: Toward a Corporeal Feminism*, Indiana University Press (Indianapolis), 1994, p23. See also, Michel Foucault, *Discipline and Punish: The Birth of the Prison*, Random House (New York), 1977 [1975].

6 Andrew Saint, *The Image of the Architect*, Yale University Press (New Haven), 1983; Robert Gutman, *Architectural Practice: A Critical View*, Princeton Architectural Press (New York), 1988; Spiro Kostof (ed), *The Architect: Chapters in the History of the Profession*, Oxford University Press (New York), 1977; Walter Gropius, *Scope of Total Architecture*, Collier Books (New York), 1962 [1943].

7 Manuel Castells, *The Informational City: Information Technology, Economic Restructuring, and the Urban Regional Process*, Blackwell Publishers (Cambridge, Mass), 1989, p6.

8 David Harvey, *The Condition of Postmodernity: An Inquiry into the Origins of Cultural Change*, Basil Blackwell (Cambridge, Mass), 1990, p156-158.

9 These transformations can be seen across architectural practice, from Rafael Viñoly's design and oversight of the Tokyo International Forum from his small office in New York (which expanded to a design team of nearly 70 individuals), to the design of the Korean Presbyterian Church of New York, through an affiliation of three small firms whose principals, Douglas Garofalo, Greg Lynn, and Michael McInturf, each work in a different city.

10 Katerina Rüedi, 'The Architect: Commodity and Seller in One', in Katerina Rüedi, et al (eds) *Desiring Practices: Architecture, Gender and the Interdisciplinary*, Black Dog Publishing Limited (London),1996, pp241-2.

11 Beatriz Colomina, 'Battle Lines: E.1027' in Francesca Hughes (ed) *The Architect: Reconstructing Her Practice*, The MIT Press (Cambridge, Mass), 1996, p6.

12 Haraway, *Simians, Cyborgs, and Women*, p164.

13 Former *Progressive Architecture* editor Thomas Fisher noted this in 1994 when he questioned whether the profession's institutions were capable of restructuring to meet the challenges of the reconstitution of architectural practice. Thomas Fisher, 'Can This Profession Be Saved?', *Progressive Architecture* 125, February 1994, pp44-49.

14 The most recent, comprehensive study of US architectural schools and their relationship to the profession and society was published as Ernest L Boyer and Lee D Mitgang, *Building Community: A New Future for Architectural Education and Practice*, The Carnegie Foundation for the Advancement of Teaching (Princeton),1996. This document has fostered considerable debate. For an analysis of the status of the profession see William S Saunders (ed) *Reflections on Architectural Practices in the Nineties*, Princeton Architectural Press (New York), 1996.

15 Crosbie's *Progressive Architecture* piece on architecture schools is a striking example of a narrow view. More recently, *Architecture* magazine took the opposite position, devoting an entire issue to education, including Reed Kroloff's 'How the Profession is Failing the Schools', *Architecture* 85, August 1996, pp94-95. *Metropolis* magazine (September 1995 and October 1997) also takes a broader approach, looking at diversity within and between schools and the variety of practices and professions that graduates ultimately pursue.

16 bell hooks, *Yearning: race, gender and cultural politics*, South End Press, (Boston), 1990, p31.

EDIBLE ARCHITECTURE
FROM AUSTRIA TO LONDON

A parking space on Greek Street, Soho, in London, has recently seen the launch of an unusual "architectural" event.

Eating Architecture - Greek Street Cake Event was the last part of a study module during which the second and third year architecture students from the Observation Studio, run by Julia Chance and Torsten Schmiedeknecht at the School of Architecture at Kingston University, were each assigned a building on Greek Street and then asked to perform a number of observational tasks on and about their individual building. The intention was to record not only the physical and material qualities of the street, but also more abstract observations, such as the manner in which the occupants perceive it, their state of mind as they walk along it, their awareness of its surfaces and atmosphere.

Working on a scale of 1:50, the students were asked to make models of each of the buildings on the street. Bearing in mind that Soho is an area where people go out to eat, drink, talk and dance, they decided on cake as an edible modelling material. They also prepared a leaflet entitled 'Eating Architecture – Greek Street Cake Event', inviting occupants to view the model and sample a taste of their building.

This idea has a precedent in the project "Urban Toys" by the Austrian Group Haus-Rucker-Co in the early nineteen-seventies. Part of the project was the recreation of Central Park within Central Park in Manhattan, New York City in 1972 as an edible model. Haus-Rucker-Co considered the city to be a public landscape that had to be cultivated.

In *Translations from Drawings to Buildings* (Architectural Association Publications, London, 1997), Robin Evans observed that students of architecture face a peculiar disadvantage in that they are 'never working directly with the object of their thought, always working at it through some intervening medium, almost always the drawing, while painters and

sculptors, who might spend some time on preliminary sketches and maquettes, all end up working on the thing itself, which naturally absorbed most of their effort and attention'.

With this in mind, the cake event aimed to position itself between art and architecture: the cakes were not only 1:50-scale representations of the built reality surrounding them, but were also handmade objects in their own right at a scale of 1:1. By endowing the street model with this dual role – on the one hand a representation of the existing urban situation and on the other a desirable object to be eaten – the students challenged the public's perception of its urban environment.

INSIDE THE FOLD
THE FORM OF FORM
Simone Brott

Folding is a formal operation used to connect disparate elements of a site (or building) in a continuous, 'multiplicitous mixture'. This tactic is not just a theoretical device. On a pragmatic level, folding can be applied to various design problems in which disparate elements need to be related in such a way that they appear seamless. It provides a new way of resolving junctions and compositions.

Folding can be considered a legitimate new style for two reasons. Firstly, it is based on a new graphics. The deconstructivist aesthetic provides fresh formal outcomes, because it combines ordinary graphic operations in non-orthogonal compositions. Alternatively, folding departs from the operations cut, rotate, divide, etc, and when used with form-generating software, is able to produce something

entirely different. This new graphics has led to new kinds of forms, and new forms are as critical to architecture as are new ideas. For Mandelbrot, odd shapes carried meaning, and for us too, these new forms mean something, even whilst revolutionary graphic freedom and formal experimentation has been trivialised by the discourse.

Finally, folding as a philosophical framework makes explicit architecture's nature as neither entirely deterministic nor entirely random. This is an obvious, but important observation. Just as chaos is different from

true randomness, folding architecture is different from truly random forms. The condition of architecture is that form is neither truly random, nor is it intrinsically meaningful, so architecture can legitimately be conceived of as pseudo-random.

If we follow this argument,

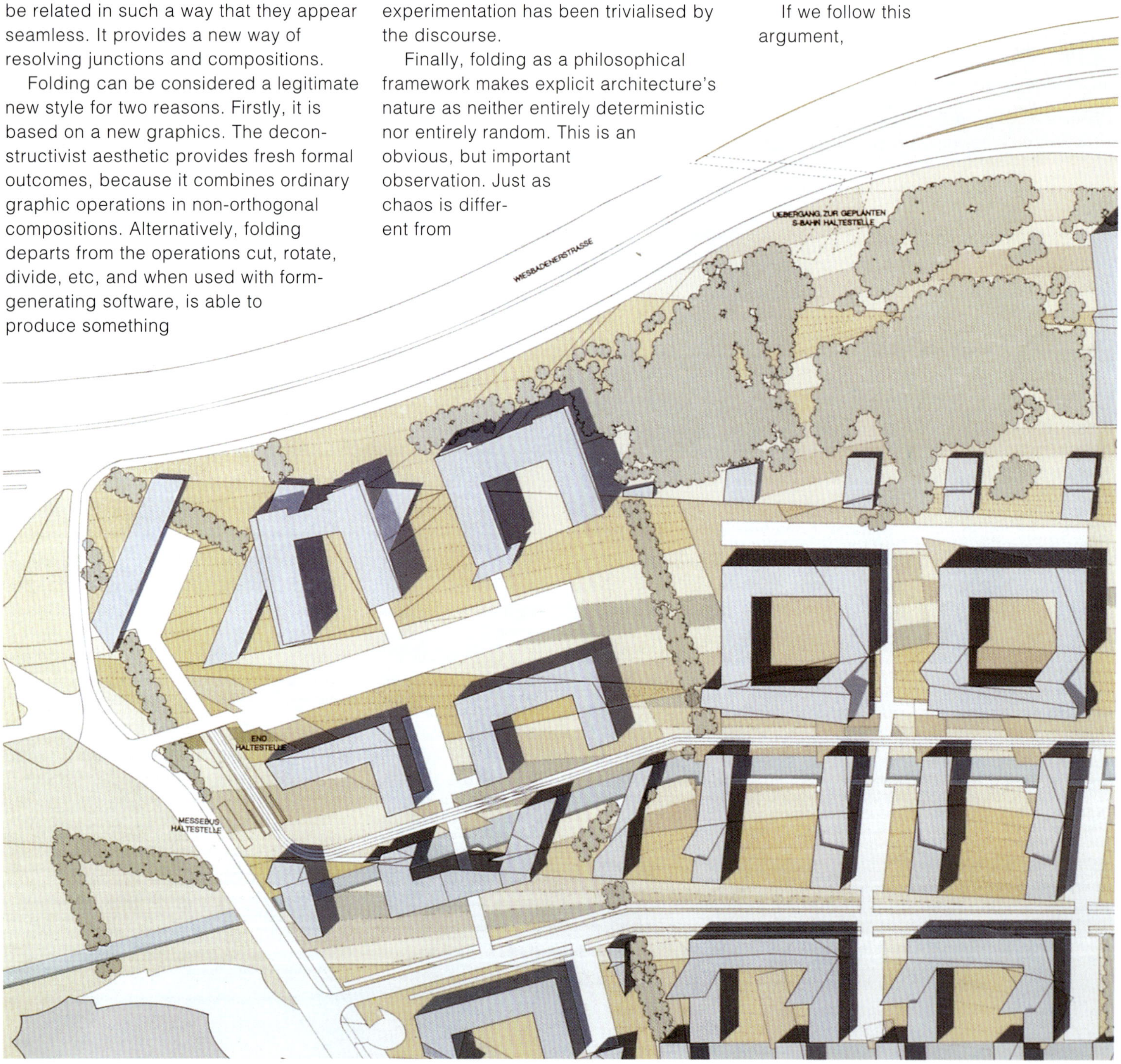

WIESBADENERSTRASSE

UEBERGANG ZUR GEPLANTEN
S-BAHN HALTESTELLE

END
HALTESTELLE

MESSEBUS
HALTESTELLE

ABOVE: Peter Eisenman, Center for the Arts, Emory University, Atlanta, concept model; OPPOSITE: Peter Eisenman, Rebstock Park, competition site plan

folding is the obvious design methodology for form generation. Those who have studied *AD* 'Folding in Architecture' (Vol 63)[1] may remember its enthusiasm for catastrophe meshes, Deleuze's fold, and technical terms such as 'inflection point' and 'topological geometry'. However, our task is not to seek technical parity between the original theories of the fold and their application in architecture, but to judge the worth of the magazine's interpretation of the fold as it is tailored towards our own discourse. Writers in this publication (including Greg Lynn, Jeffrey Kipnis, John Rajchman et al) engaged in a criticism of so-called 'Postmodern tactics' of collage and discordance in favour of a smoother architecture of folding.[2]

The argument for a new folding architecture goes something like this: Postmodernist architecture was a reaction against Modernism in architecture. For this polemic to work architects had to utilise 'jagged discordances' and collage. The work had to be both formally heterogeneous and outwardly subversive, whatever that might be. The criticisms against Deconstructivist architecture, combined with Lynn's claim that architects are no longer intent on expressing the differences or contradictions of a site, call for a new way of relating architectural elements. To quote Lynn, the architect at the end of the 20th century 'faces the problem of reconciling the opposing goals of conflict and contradiction [of Postmodernism] and [Modernism's goal] of unity and reconstruction'.[3]

What Lynn suggests as the formal alternative to collage, of course, is the fold. The idea then, is to integrate the unrelated elements of both the site and programme in a 'smooth, pliant multiplicitous mixture'. The concept of folding is appealing to these theorists because it allows for discontinuities, but in a continuous rather than discordant way. In other words, it achieves continuous discontinuity. Further, not only should elements be made to pass into each

other, but the forms also respond to each other. This can be achieved, he claims, by employing topological geometry to produce folded surfaces that are mutable and pliant.

Against this background, let us look at some built projects promoted in that issue of *AD*. Peter Eisenman's Rebstock Park Project is an urban housing project in Frankfurt. Eisenman defines the historical architectural context in Frankfurt as the typical perimeter housing and commercial block of German cities. In the mid-19th century came the development of the *siedlung* – multi-storey, linear block row housing.[4] Eisenman claims that both urbanisms treat the buildings as foreground objects, rendering the ground as a kind of left-over space. With Rebstock, he attempts to revise the *siedlung* urban typology by ensuring that the buildings are folded into the ground and that the ground is itself folded. Furthermore, he claims that the building is not an object or a point in space as in a Cartesian grid: 'The smallest element is no longer the point but the fold'.[5]

If we look at the master plan, it is difficult to observe these items. The ground may not have been flattened but the master plan is still effectively a figure-ground diagram of objects within a tightly composed grid. There is no evidence of folding.[6]

Another example is Bahram Shirdel's Nara Convention Centre in Japan. The architects state: 'Our goal for the Nara Convention Centre is to weave the three principal functions of a major civic building – the aesthetic/symbolic relationship to cultural context, the relationship to the immediate site, and the programmatic experience – into a complex spatial unity guided by the theme of the symbiosis of history and the future'.[7]

The elements of this building do not form a complex unity that we can observe. Rather, the junctions of its elements and the overall massing give the impression of a Deconstructivist building. However, some of the images would indicate self-similarity in the forms, and a self-recursive massing.

In Greg Lynn's Stranded Sears Tower, we can also see evidence of folding. This project takes the Sears Tower, which Lynn describes as a vertical group of nine towers, and reformulates the image of the American monument by laying the building on its side and straining it into 2,025 strands, which are made to participate with their immediate context in a 'supple and pliant manner.' 'The strands exploit possible connections with and between adjacent buildings, sidewalks, bridges, tunnels and landforms'.[8] Lynn claims that the reconfigured tower is no longer a monolith, that it is irreducible to any single type. One could respond that while it may not take on the form of a monument in the traditional sense, it dominates its context nonetheless. This is a super structure that is neither pliant nor responsive to its context.

Lynn points out the most obvious criticism of folding as a style: '... despite protestations to the contrary, it is more than likely that Thom's catastrophe nets entered into the architecture of Carsten Juel-Christiansen's Die Anhalter Faltung, Peter Eisenman's Rebstock Park, Jeffrey Kipnis' Unite de Habitation at Briey installation and Bahram Shirdel's Nara Convention Hall as a mere formal technique... it is precisely the formal manipulations of folding that are capable of incorporating manifold external forces and elements within form, yet Le Pli undoubtedly risks being translated into architecture as mere folded figures'.[9] He suggests that we should produce not a style, but a practice, of folding.[10]

Another weakness of this surface architecture, is that it often lacks human scale. An example is Frank Gehry's Guggenheim Museum in Bilbao. The defining feature of Mandelbrot's pattern is the rule combined with the starting number or position. Thus, there is no hierarchy. No matter how large an area we focus on, the pattern merely reproduces itself. We could invert this argument by claiming that the pattern exhibits itself no matter how small. And this is perhaps what folding architecture is currently lacking – complexity on different scales. A folding operation frees up the surface for new kinds of expression, but without complexity we lack human scale, human interest, and the result is similar to the monuments of Modernism. A blank wall, 20 metres high interrupted by a fold is not really any more interesting than a 20-metre-high blank wall. Authentic folding is described as folds within folds. What is also required is more use of pattern, texture, and play of colours – a richer version of folding.

Storey Hall is successful not because of its theoretical concerns, but because it boasts a high degree of aesthetic complexity for its small scale. Further, it respects the idea that a person is a certain height, and that openings and windows should correspond to one's field of vision. The Corrigan building, next

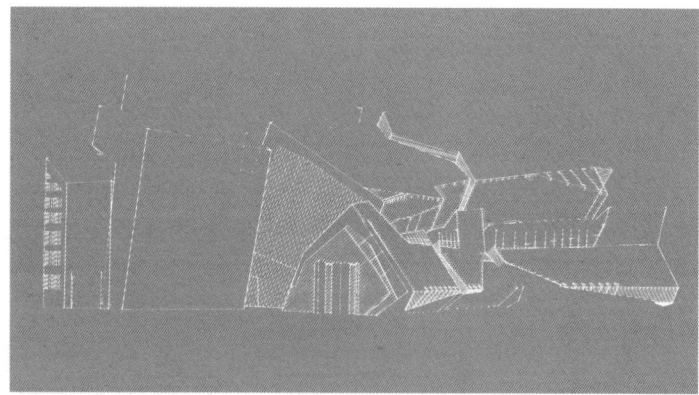 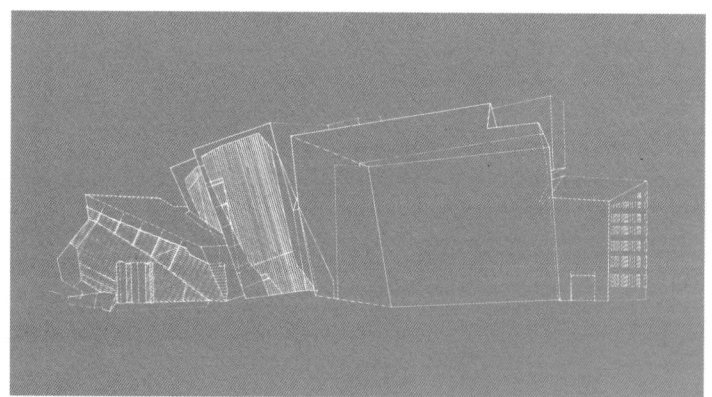

Bahram Shirdel, Nara Convention Hall, Japan, south and north elevations

door, is similarly complex and interesting (whet-her you like it or not). It is not an example of folding, but it really is interested in its street. There is richness for people to engage with as they walk alongside the building. The Guggenheim in Bilbao, on the other hand, is a monument, a rise to power. It has no concern for people, scale, or context.

We need to understand the agenda behind a style that attempts to promote multiplicitous unity. Why should we aim for unity or continuity? To answer this question we must look at the background of folding. It seems that Deconstruction, as the architecture of difference and discontinuity produced by and for Postmodern consumption and popular in the 80s,[11] was replaced at the beginning of this decade by a new commodity – continuity. In other words, we seem to be arching back towards a quasi-Modernist idealisation of unity and continuity. However, not admitting to being rationalists, or submissive Modernists, we sublimate with the term 'multiplicitous continuity'. This is the appearance of discontinuities in a continuous mix; a complex continuity. Lynn deploys this rhetoric with adjectives like 'submissive' or 'compliant': 'forms will now be pliable, compliant, they will adapt, to external forces', he states.[12] This carries a very odd tone. Clearly, it is humans, and not buildings that comply or submit. This theory appeals to a strange power subjugation. Folding may afford a new kind of freedom to architects both graphically and formally, but it is politically deficient.[13]

Notes

1 *Architectural Design*, 'Folding in Architecture', Andreas Papadakis (ed), Academy Editions (London), 1993.
2 Greg Lynn, 'Architectural Curvilinearity. The Folded, the Pliant and the Supple', ibid, p8.
3 Greg Lynn, op cit, p8.
4 Peter Eisenman, 'Folding in Time. The Singularity of Rebstock', in *AD*, 'Folding in Architecture', pp23-4.
5 Ibid, p25.
6 Eisenman's Alteka Office Building in Japan is more clear as a folding practice, particularly in its treatment of the junction between the building and the ground.
7 Bahram Shirdel, 'Nara Convention Hall', *AD*, 'Folding in Architecture', p51.
8 Greg Lynn, 'Stranded Sears Tower', *AD*, 'Folding in Architecture', p83.
9 Greg Lynn, 'Architectural Curvilinearity. The Folded, the Pliant and the Supple', *AD*, 'Folding in Architecture', p13.
10 Lynn, op cit.
11 by Venturi, Wigley et al.
12 Lynn, op cit
13 The politics of Post-Structuralism. Lynn claims that Deconstruction was a reaction against Modernism and that folding attempts a synthesis of their architectural goals. This may be the appropriate response, architecturally, but can we – or should we – ignore the politics of Poststructuralist Theory, namely, the subtle agenda of Derrida (and many others in cultural theory) of exposing the suppressed term in a binary opposition. There is no evidence to suggest that this project has been completed.

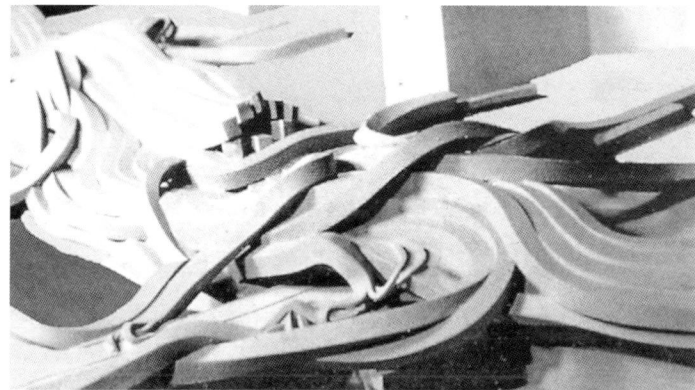

Greg Lynn, Stranded Sears Tower, model views

MORE FOR INSPIRATION ONLY

Future Systems

More For Inspiration Only is a continuation of the highly successful, visually explosive *For Inspiration Only*, published in 1996. Jan Kaplicky of Future Systems – a practice synonymous with architecturally pioneering and technologically creative design – presents many more of his rich, eclectic sources of inspiration from around the world.

For this second book in the series he has chosen images of nature, technology, planes, cars, graphics, people, colours, fashion, planets. The sources are endless, ranging from a Cycladic sculpture, to a London bus ticket, or a fly's eye. 'It's sometimes frightening for me how much man or nature can achieve. Architecture and design is of course only a marginal fraction of all this', Kaplicky explains. 'Here is proof that creativity is absolutely essential all the time'. He believes that the inspiration for architecture should be limitless in order to enable architects to produce fresh solutions to the issue of living space. 'I pity people who can't see all this richness', he continues. 'Millions of people have eyes, only a few can use them. This book is for them.'

A section of the book shows a direct link between Kaplicky's source of inspiration and his projects: aerials on a M 998 Jeep juxtaposed with Project 246 Construction Tower Pendulum; a submarine alongside Project 175 Boatel, for example. For Future Systems these connections are an essential and natural part of the everyday creative process. Kaplicky concludes, 'If one student of architecture, design or engineering can use this book, I'll be a happy man'.

PB 0 471 98770 0; 140x 140 mm; 128 pages; March 1999

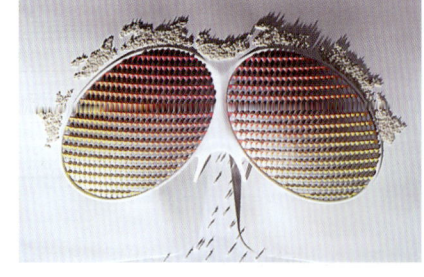

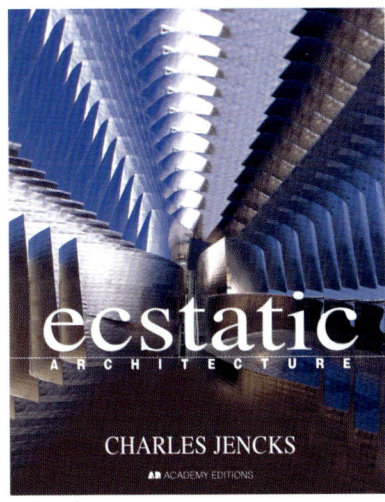

ECSTATIC ARCHITECTURE

Charles Jencks

For most of this century, architects have felt the need to justify every design they make, every line they draw, according to the basic principles of modernist functionalism. This book examines the backlash: the current top architects are seeking not to theorise their work, but to enjoy it. As this shift transcends architectural styles, architects are at last free to indulge their true and highly personal motivations. Admission of visual preferences, dreams, narratives, contingencies and even budgets as the real reasons for design decisions, are now considered acceptable.

The critic Charles Jencks has termed this new freedom 'Ecstatic Architecture'. Stimulating, holistic, often ritualistic and overpowering, its primary contemporary monument is Frank Gehry's New Guggenheim Museum in Bilbao, which has caused such widespread acclaim and rethinking of assumptions that it has given birth to a new genre: 'Bilbaoism'.

Through a series of extensive photo essays, Jencks shows not only how the Ecstatic is opening up current architectural thought, but that it follows on from historic precedents. He traces links between the current practice of leading architects such as Hans Hollein, Coop Himmelb(l)au and Nigel Coates, and Egyptian, Baroque and Art Nouveau architecture. He argues that the Ecstatic illuminates buildings widely distant in function and time, from cave art to the new cinema centre in Dresden, from explicitly erotic architecture to buildings that have a spiritual role, from Conceptual and cybernetic artefacts to pure architecture.

In a series of essays Paolo Portoghesi, Maggie Toy and Neil Leach discuss the historic and philosophical implications of this notion. Major projects in the genre by leading practitioners including Frank Gehry, Will Alsop, Ron Arad, Odile Decq, Eric Moss, Hans Hollein and Shin Takamatsu are included.

PB 0 471 98398 5; 276 x 216 mm; 176 pages; April 1999

FRANK LLOYD WRIGHT: FIELD GUIDE, VOL 3

Thomas A Heinz

This is the third of four volumes in a series that provides the first comprehensive visitors' guide to all of Frank Lloyd Wright's buildings in the United States. Each guide is written and compiled by Thomas A Heinz, an acknowledged expert on Wright. In his highly readable and informative style, Heinz presents each building page by page, providing brief histories and background details, information on accessibility and viewing, and directions from Interstate routes. Every entry is accompanied by a colour photograph and location map.

The four volumes in the *Field Guide* series each deal with a different geographical location: Upper Great Lakes, Chicago, West and East. Arranged according to area, they begin in the northwest and end in the southeast of the region covered. Full alphabetical and geographical lists enable buildings to be easily accessed either by location or name. In this volume, Heinz leads us to the west, a highlight of which is the Conrad Edward Gordon House in Wilsonville, Oregon.

PB 0 471 97747 0; 200 x 135; 168 pages; April 1999

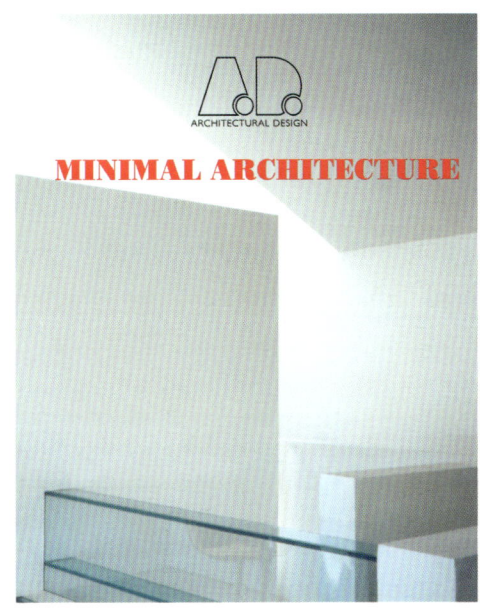

MINIMAL ARCHITECTURE

AD Profile No 139

Edited by Maggie Toy

Minimal Architecture is a follow-up to the sell-out success of 'Aspects of Minimal Architecture'. This design philosophy reflects the desire for a reductivist, uncluttered way of life, a search for calm and tranquil environments. Its designers can trace their inspiration back to the Modern Movement.

The results of this style are stunningly beautiful and very popular. Leading architectural designers discussed in this issue include John Pawson, Claudio Silvestrin, Deborah Berke, Richard Gluckman, David Chipperfield, Edward Souta de Moura, Peter Zumthor, Herzog & de Meuron.

PB 0 471 98859 6, 305 x 252 mm; 112 pages; May/June 1999

Reviews Books

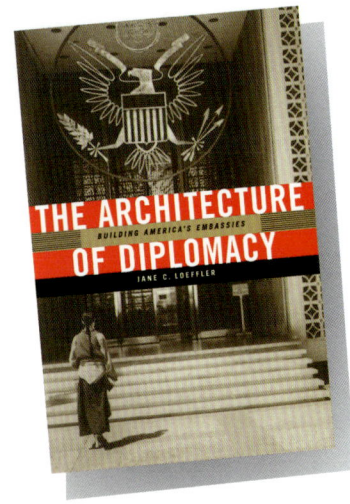

Frank O. Gehry
Guggenheim Bilbao Museoa

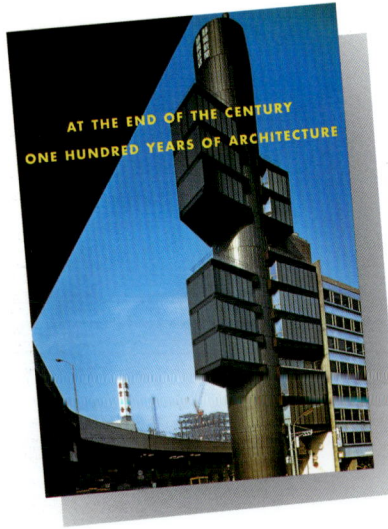

The Architecture of Diplomacy: Building America's Embassies, *by Jane C Loeffler, Princeton Architectural Press (New York), 404pp, b/w ills, HB £19.95*

Embassies are visual statements of a country's projected self-image. Jane C Loeffler's book seems to suggest that there is no act more political or architecturally complicated than building an embassy. This is a building type about which remarkably little has been written. Loeffler has braved the red tape and brought us a precise, accessible narrative on these manifestations of global foreign policy.

Embassies are the vehicles through which countries have chosen to reassert themselves in a post-war, post-colonial world. Loeffler traces their development from mid-century modern glass buildings, in which openness and accessibility were both diplomatic and artistic objectives, to later, more imposing buildings, in which the architectural style was subordinated to many other factors. She demonstrates how expressive a role embassies play in revealing the conditions and demands of a rapidly changing and increasingly threatening world. By the mid-60s, due to the rise in terrorism and espionage, security was more often the priority and the streams of Vietnam protestors ensured that the modern, inviting structures were no longer practical; necessity dictated that the embassies promote a more intimidating fortress-like image.

Frank O Gehry: Guggenheim Bilbao Museoa, *introduced by Kurt W Forster, Edition Axel Menges GmbH, 56pp, colour ills, HB £24.00*

Frank Gehry's Guggenheim Museum in Bilbao shows how much impact cleverly commissioned architecture can have. The building is the central element in Bilbao's comprehensive urban renewal programme. Its site between river, railway, bridge and new town makes it a Basque symbol that can be seen from a considerable distance. The project was intended to be both the heart of the city and a testbed for the arts, representing public presence and artistic change.

The process by which the museum was created demonstrates the most recent advances in computer-aided design, and in material manufacture. For many years, design and building were broken down into a large number of individual components. Gehry's museum unifies this process and is thus able to create fluent links between ar-

chitectural detail and urban impact.

One of the most unusual aspects of this project is the way in which the interior spaces are shaped. These are extremely varied in form, reflecting the fact that the museum is not so much designed to house a permanent exhibition of the collection, but to enable artists to create installations. In contrast to the customary neutral gallery spaces, Gehry offers a wide variety of stages for artistic presentation. His artist friends have risen to the challenge of his architecture and are experimenting very successfully with this new way of showing their work to the public.

At the End of the Century: One Hundred Years of Architecture, *organised by Richard Koshalek and Elizabeth AT Smith, Mocha (Abrams), 336pp, colour ills, HB £40.00*

This enormous catalogue for the exhibition at the Museum of Contemporary Art, Los Angeles, sponsored by the Ford Motor Company, is physically weighty but what of its content? As Richard Koshalek states in his foreword, this is an ambitious project, but 'despite the size and scope of the exhibition, it is not exhaustive, nor does it encompass all the canonical works of architecture that might be expected in a more conventional survey. Instead, it offers a way to consider the present by examining key developments of the past and suggests implications for the future in terms of the power of architecture and urbanism to shape and reflect our cultures and ways of life'.

As every self-respecting publisher rushes to produce its own 'end-of-millennium' book, it is a refreshing change to note that this volume has employed more than one author. Each chapter is worthy of a book in itself, covering topical issues of globalism and the much neglected south of America in a chapter entitled 'Latin America: The Places of the Other'.

In her essay 'Re-examining Architecture and its History at the End of the Century', Elizabeth AT Smith claims of this exhibition, 'rather than foregrounding a series of singular architectural achievements, it positions them within a context of related works – built and unbuilt – and ideas, many of which are considerably lesser known even to the architecture community'. Many of the old favourites are included, however. It was no surprise to find that Adolf Loos' Moller House, Vienna (1928),

Reviews
Books

opens the chapter by Beatriz Colomina on 'The Exhibitionist House', for example. But on the whole, this publication succeeds in punctuating the more obvious examples with less classic work such as the Okada Residence, Omori, Tokyo, by Sutemi Horiguchi (1933), which can be found at the start of an enlightening chapter on internationalism versus regionalism by Hajime Yatsuka.

Pacific Edge: Contemporary Architecture on the Pacific Rim*, by Peter Zellner with essays by Aaron Betsky, Davina Jackson and Akira Suzuki, Thames and Hudson Ltd (London), 224pp, colour ills, HB £32.00*
As Herman Melville writes in *Moby Dick*, 'Thus this mysterious divine Pacific zones the whole world's bulk around it; make all coasts one bay to it; seems the tide-beating heart of the earth'. It is, indeed, an ambitious book that attempts to cover 35 countries, encompassing East Asian, Polynesian, American, Melanesian, South-east Asian, Latin American and Australasian cultures. Naturally, much of the writing presents various angles on the idea of unity in the region: Aaron Betsky's introduction to 'Collage Cities, Homes beyond the Range' focuses on the cities of western America, where he claims 'you will find yourself confronting signs in every possible language and in every shape and colour'. This subjugation of one culture to another he describes as 'the ultimate logic of urbanisation itself'.

This is a timely publication, not only because the region is developing faster than the speed with which people are able to evaluate it, but also because these architects represent a new approach to design, integrating diverse elements to produce something entirely unexpected and yet characteristic of very different places.

Lloyd Wright: The Architecture of Frank Lloyd Wright Jr*, by Alan Weintraub, Thames and Hudson Ltd (London), 275pp, colour ills, HB £40.00*
The easiest way to get through this genealogical minefield is to turn to page 228, on which there is a picture entitled 'LW, FLW and ELW at Wingspread c1937': three generations of 'LW's and three generations of architects. Once grasped, the constant references to father and son fall into place.

Both FLW's son LW (Frank Lloyd Wright Jr, referred to as Lloyd Wright) and his grandson ELW (Eric) worked in FLW's office for a time. The pressure of being forever in the great man's shadow might have encouraged them to branch out and do something completely different, but they both developed a remarkably similar approach to architecture. There are some exquisite drawings that demonstrate Frank Lloyd Wright's influence over his son. The 1959 sketch for the Dejonghe house in particular has a sturdy elegance typical of the master. In the final chapter, 'Lloyd Wright's Studio – A Son's Reflections', by Eric Lloyd Wright, Frank Lloyd Wright's grandson recalls his father's 'superb sense of space – of when to let "emptiness" alone speak', a quality that has often been associated with FLW himself.

Anaïs Nin, an acquaintance of LW's from the 1940s wrote, 'He is the poet of architecture. For him a building, a home, a stone, a roof, every inch of architecture has meaning'.

This publication joins a new genre of books in which the front cover is graced soley by the name of the architectural photographer. Weintraub has painstakingly documented Lloyd Wright's work. Although he must have known that anything on this subject would be lapped up by the architectural press, the publication is fully justified by the quality of the work inside.

The Metropolis of Tomorrow, *by Hugh Ferriss, Princeton Architectural Press (New York), 200pp, b/w ills, HB £25.00*
From the 1920s through to the 1950s Hugh Ferriss was America's most celebrated architectural artist, serving as consulting architect for the 1934 New York World's Fair and for the United Nations Headquarters. This book was first published in 1929. It is considered to be the quintessential document of the prosperity of the 1920s, as well as a personal manifesto of visionary urbanism.

Here, Carol Willis, author of *Form Follows Finance*, also published by Princeton, provides an insightful essay into what motivated Ferriss to record the cityscape as he did. His dramatic charcoal renderings present a visual discussion of the role of the American skyscraper, along with his vision for an ideal metropolis of some 20 to 50 years in the future. Included are the buildings he drew in St Louis, Chicago, New York, Detroit and LA.

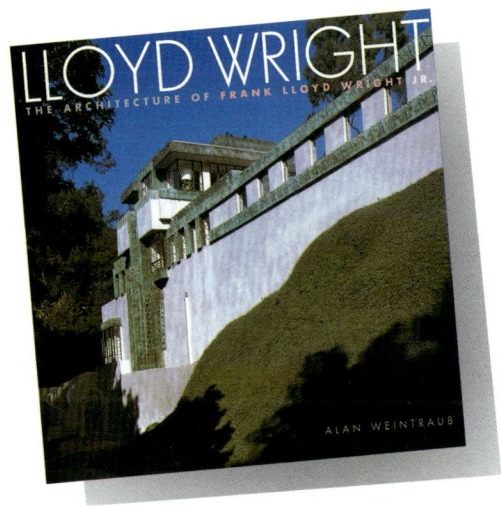

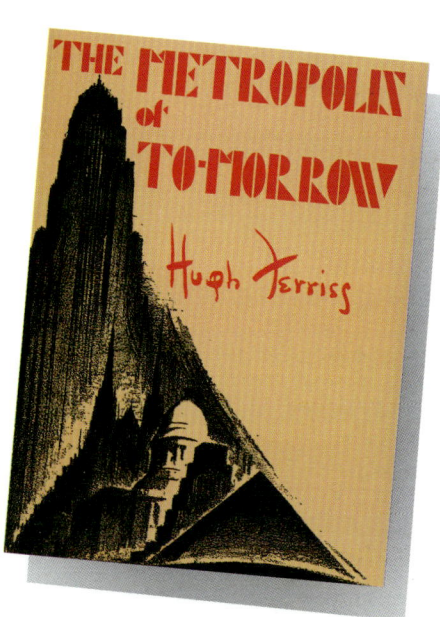

Reviews
Books

Aldo Van Eyck: The Shape of Relativity *by Francis Strauven, Architectural & Natura, (Amsterdam), 679pp, b/w & colour ills, HB £35.00*

This biography has been long awaited, to the virtual exclusion of all else about Van Eyck. The suspense has been frustrating, but the result is all that could have been wished for.

Looking back on such projects as the Municipal Orphanage of Amsterdam, it is clear how inextricable social necessity and public architecture were for Van Eyck. Only practice would prove the point. He emphasised the abiding presence of a classical tradition (which he characterised as 'immutability and rest'), yet interwove it with traditions of modernity and spontaneity (which he referred to as the 'vernacular of the heart').

Van Eyck dwelt within the poetics of architecture and yet throughout his remarkably long career his feet have remained firmly on the ground. At the Orphanage, he saw the Classical tradition as chiefly engaged within the primary organisational field, yet itself dependent upon specific retroactive processes, such as 'inside-outside' dynamics, immutability and 'centrality-dispersal'. Oppositions are set up creatively, yet attuned to one another in a kind of endless harmony.

Van Eyck long benefited from an unflinching recognition of his talents, ideas, and buildings in the pages of *Architectural Design*, which was the first journal to bring the Orphanage to public acclaim internationally. As Robert Maxwell was to add in the *Sunday Times* Magazine (29 September 1963), the Orphanage 'can have a meaning for the connoisseur and also for the immediate user – however humble – different orders of meaning but not exclusive of each other'.

Van Eyck's own writings have never been published in a collected form, though 'The Child, The City and The Artist' was a famous text, circulated throughout the United States, privately and in school circles.

Proceeding onto controversial, yet seemingly justifiable territory, Strauven claims that other critics may have absorbed Van Eyck's philosophies without due acknowledgement. In Charles Jencks' *Modern Movements in Architecture*, Van Eyck's attitude to 'place' is adopted without reservation. The other authors cited are Christopher Alexander, Christian Norberg-Schultz and Robert Venturi. The latter is frankly outspoken about the importance to him of Van Eyck, and this is born out in Vincent Scully's own introduction to the 1963 edition of Complexity and Contradiction.

Was Van Eyck therefore to be labelled a forerunner of the postmodern? Strauven is at pains to correct any misconceptions, while nonetheless ensuring that the actual currency of Van Eyck's thinking was instrumental here. With notable clarity he is able to pick his way through Eisenman's relationship with Van Eyck's argument that modern architecture was devoid of the true modern sensibility that emerged around the turn of the century, as Eisenman claimed, and Van Eyck foresaw in the 1950s. But in seeking the full autonomy of form, the conclusions that Eisenman drew from this generality took him in a wholly different direction.

Van Eyck's teaching influence is carefully documented by the author, who reveals the extent to which contemporary Dutch pre-eminence in design owes a massive, yet as always in academia, intangible debt to Van Eyck. As with Leslie Martin, and undoubtedly with Aalto, the strands of such a pervasive capacity to influence the thinking of a whole sector of the profession are widely spread, and still continuing.

What is remarkable in such a small-format publication, is the degree to which all key projects are documented in such a way as to do them full justice. In this respect, the author has achieved more than has been done for Aalto in four volumes. Of course, Van Eyck's oeuvre is smaller, and there is less anecdotal entertainment to divert one, but the critical assessments are invariably sound and comprehensive, whether plotting the growth of Van Eyck's concept of relativity in architecture through his schemes, or examining his development of a carefully measured yet poetic realisation of what is necessitated by 'contextuality'.

This is a monograph about an 'architect's architect'. But this magisterial tome, revealing the development of the subject from an intellectual childhood in Hampstead into a genius of global significance, cannot be merely for the benefit of fellow architects. This is a work of literary excellence and scholarship that can be enjoyed by everyone.

Michael Spens

ARCHITECTURAL DESIGN
SUBSCRIPTION RATES

SIX DOUBLE ISSUES A YEAR

Architectural Design continues to publish a lively and wide-ranging selection of cutting-edge architectural projects. Frequently in the forefront of theoretical developments in the architectural field, *AD* engenders an awareness of philosophy in art and architecture whilst always maintaining a pluralist approach. The treatment of the divergent subjects examined over the years has had a profound impact on architectural debate, making *AD* an invaluable record of architectural thinking, criticism and building.

ARCHITECTURAL DESIGN SUBSCRIPTION RATES

	UK	OUTSIDE UK
Institutional rate	£ 135.00	US$ 225.00
Personal rate	£ 90.00	US$ 145.00
Airmail prices on application		

PRICES REFLECT RATES FOR A 1999 SUBSCRIPTION
AND ARE SUBJECT TO CHANGE WITHOUT NOTICE

Back numbers are available. For more information see over.

FORTHCOMING ISSUES

VOL 69 5/6 1999 .... Minimal Architecture

VOL 69 7/8 1999 .... Architecture of the Borderlands

MINIMAL ARCHITECTURE

Explores the construction of silence and the philosophies of the reactonary minimalists

Investigates the condition of the built environment between cultural borders

VOL 69 9/10 1999 .... Hypersurface II

VOL 69 11/12 1999 ...Architecture of the Millennium Celebrations

Please complete and return this form with your payment (to be made payable to John Wiley & Sons Ltd) or credit card authority direct to:

OUTSIDE UK Subscriptions (US$)
John Wiley & Sons, Inc
Journals Administration Department
605 Third Avenue
New York, NY 10158, USA
Tel: 212 850 6645; Fax: 212 850 6021
Cable Jonwile; Telex: 12-7063
E-mail: subinfo@jwiley.com

UK Subscriptions (£)
John Wiley & Sons Ltd
Journals Administration Department
1 Oldlands Way, Bognor Regis
West Sussex, PO22 9SA, UK
Tel: 01243 843272; Fax: 01243 843232
E-mail: cs-journals@wiley.co.uk

ACADEMY EDITIONS
A division of John Wiley & Sons
42 Leinster Gardens, London W2 3AN Tel: 0171 262 5097 Fax: 0171 262 5093

ARCHITECTURAL DESIGN

☐ I wish to subscribe to *Architectural Design* at the institutional rate
☐ I wish to subscribe to *Architectural Design* at the personal rate

Starting date: from issue 1/2 1999

.... **Payment enclosed by Cheque/ Money Order/ Drafts**
Value/Currency £/US$...
.... **Please charge** £/US$.................................**to my credit card**

Account no:

Expiry date:

Card: Visa/Amex/Mastercard/Eurocard (*delete as applicable*)

Cardholder's signature...
Cardholder's name...
Address...
....**Post/Zip Code:**.................

Recipient's name..
Address...
....**Post/Zip Code:**.................

Please indicate your job title

☐ Architect
☐ Landscape Architect
☐ Architectural Technician/Assistant
☐ Surveyor
☐ Building Services Engineer
☐ Town Planner
☐ Interior Designer
☐ Designer
☐ Building Contractor
☐ Property Developer
☐ Student (*state college/university below*)
☐ Other (*state below*)

Please indicate your organisation

☐ Private practice
☐ Local authority
☐ Public/Government department
☐ Contractor
☐ Industrial/Commercial company
☐ Research establishment
☐ College/University (*state below*)
☐ Other (*state below*)

ARCHITECTURAL DESIGN

☐ I wish to subscribe to *Architectural Design* at the institutional rate
☐ I wish to subscribe to *Architectural Design* at the personal rate

Starting date: from issue 1/2 1999

.... **Payment enclosed by Cheque/ Money Order/ Drafts**
Value/Currency £/US$...
.... **Please charge** £/US$.................................**to my credit card**

Account no:

Expiry date:

Card: Visa/Amex/Mastercard/Eurocard (*delete as applicable*)

Cardholder's signature...
Cardholder's name...
Address...
....**Post/Zip Code:**.................

Recipient's name..
Address...
....**Post/Zip Code:**.................

Please indicate your job title

☐ Architect
☐ Landscape Architect
☐ Architectural Technician/Assistant
☐ Surveyor
☐ Building Services Engineer
☐ Town Planner
☐ Interior Designer
☐ Designer
☐ Building Contractor
☐ Property Developer
☐ Student (*state college/university below*)
☐ Other (*state below*)

Please indicate your organisation

☐ Private practice
☐ Local authority
☐ Public/Government department
☐ Contractor
☐ Industrial/Commercial company
☐ Research establishment
☐ College/University (*state below*)
☐ Other (*state below*)

ARCHITECTURAL DESIGN

☐ I wish to subscribe to *Architectural Design* at the institutional rate
☐ I wish to subscribe to *Architectural Design* at the personal rate

Starting date: from issue 1/2 1999

.... **Payment enclosed by Cheque/ Money Order/ Drafts**
Value/Currency £/US$...
.... **Please charge** £/US$.................................**to my credit card**

Account no:

Expiry date:

Card: Visa/Amex/Mastercard/Eurocard (*delete as applicable*)

Cardholder's signature...
Cardholder's name...
Address...
....**Post/Zip Code:**.................

Recipient's name..
Address...
....**Post/Zip Code:**.................

Please indicate your job title

☐ Architect
☐ Landscape Architect
☐ Architectural Technician/Assistant
☐ Surveyor
☐ Building Services Engineer
☐ Town Planner
☐ Interior Designer
☐ Designer
☐ Building Contractor
☐ Property Developer
☐ Student (*state college/university below*)
☐ Other (*state below*)

Please indicate your organisation

☐ Private practice
☐ Local authority
☐ Public/Government department
☐ Contractor
☐ Industrial/Commercial company
☐ Research establishment
☐ College/University (*state below*)
☐ Other (*state below*)

PLEASE CROSS THOSE BACK NUMBERS THAT YOU ARE INTERESTED IN

24	72	74	77	84	100	102	109	110	112	117	118
120	123	124	125	126	127						

I am interested in the above marked back numbers. Please quote me a special price for back numbers of this magazine.

Name: _____

Address: _____

_____

Post/Zip code: _____

ACADEMY EDITIONS
A division of John Wiley & Sons
42 Leinster Gardens, London W2 3AN Tel: 0171 262 5097 Fax: 0171 262 5093

PLEASE CROSS THOSE BACK NUMBERS THAT YOU ARE INTERESTED IN

24	72	74	77	84	100	102	109	110	112	117	118
120	123	124	125	126	127						

I am interested in the above marked back numbers. Please quote me a special price for back numbers of this magazine.

Name: _____

Address: _____

_____

Post/Zip code: _____

ACADEMY EDITIONS
A division of John Wiley & Sons
42 Leinster Gardens, London W2 3AN Tel: 0171 262 5097 Fax: 0171 262 5093

PLEASE CROSS THOSE BACK NUMBERS THAT YOU ARE INTERESTED IN

24	72	74	77	84	100	102	109	110	112	117	118
120	123	124	125	126	127						

I am Interested In the above marked back numbers. Please quote me a special price for back numbers of this magazine.

Name: _____

Address: _____

_____

Post/Zip code: _____

ACADEMY EDITIONS
A division of John Wiley & Sons
42 Leinster Gardens, London W2 3AN Tel: 0171 262 5097 Fax: 0171 262 5093

AD 127 ARCHITECTURE AFTER GEOMETRY
AD 126 LIGHT IN ARCHITECTURE
AD 125 ARCHITECTURE OF ECOLOGY
AD 124 ARCHITECTURE AND ANTHROPOLOGY
AD 123 INTEGRATING ARCHITECTURE
AD 121 GAMES IN THE PROCESS OF ARCHITECTURE*
AD 120 COLOUR IN ARCHITECTURE
AD 119 BEYOND THE REVOLUTION*
AD 118 ARCHITECTS IN CYBERSPACE
AD 117 TENSILE STRUCTURES
AD 116 REACHING FOR THE SKIES*
AD 115 BRITISH ARCHITECTS IN EXILE*
AD 114 THE POWER OF ARCHITECTURE*
AD 113 ARCHITECTURE AND WATER*
AD 112 ARCHITECTURE AND FILM
AD 111 NEW TOWNS*
AD 110 ASPECTS OF MINIMAL ARCHITECTURE
AD 109 ARCHITECTURE OF TRANSPORTATION
AD 108 THE PERIPHERY*
AD 107 JAPANESE ARCHITECTURE III*
AD 106 CONTEMPORARY ORGANIC ARCHITECTURE*
AD 105 NEW PRACTICE IN URBAN DESIGN*
AD 104 VISIONS FOR THE FUTURE*
AD 103 ARCHITECTURE IN ARCADIA*
AD 102 FOLDING IN ARCHITECTURE
AD 101 ARCHITECTURE AND THE ENVIRONMENT*
AD IH INTERVENTIONS IN HISTORIC CENTRES (SPECIAL PROFILE)*
AD 100 THEORY AND EXPERIMENTATION
AD 99 JAPANESE ARCHITECTURE II*
AD 98 POP ARCHITECTURE*
AD 97 PATERNOSTER SQUARE*
AD 96 FREE SPACE ARCHITECTURE*
AD 95 MODERN PLURALISM*
AD 94 NEW MUSEUMS*
AD 93 THE AVANT-GARDE*
AD 92 BERLIN TOMORROW*
AD 91 POST-MODERN TRIUMPHS IN LONDON*
AD 90 ASPECTS OF MODERN ARCHITECTURE*
AD 89 A NEW SPIRIT IN ARCHITECTURE*
AD 88 POST-MODERNISM ON TRIAL*
AD 87 DECONSTRUCTION III*
AD 86 THE NEW MODERN AESTHETIC*
AD 85 JAMES STIRLING, MICHAEL WILFORD & ASSOCIATES*
AD 84 NEW ARCHITECTURE NEW EDITION
AD 83 URBAN CONCEPTS*
AD 82 WEXNER CENTER*
AD 81 RECONSTRUCTION/DECONSTRUCTION NEW EDITION *
AD 80 RUSSIAN CONSTRUCTIVISM & IAKOV CHERNIKHOV*
AD 79 PRINCE CHARLES & THE ARCHITECTURAL DEBATE*
AD 78 DRAWING INTO ARCHITECTURE*
AD 77 DECONSTRUCTION II NEW EDITION
AD 76 NEW DIRECTIONS IN CURRENT ARCHITECTURE*
AD 75 IMITATION & INNOVATION*
AD 74 CONTEMPORARY ARCHITECTURE
AD 73 JAPANESE ARCHITECTURE*
AD 72 DECONSTRUCTION IN ARCHITECTURE NEW EDITION
AD 24 BRITAIN IN THE THIRTIES

*Please order marked issues from:
Grange Books Plc
The Grange
Grange Yard
London SE1 3AG
UK

SCI-FI ARCHITECTURE

SHUHEI ENDO, ROOFTECTURE, HYOGO PREFECTURE, JAPAN

Architectural Design

SCI-FI ARCHITECTURE

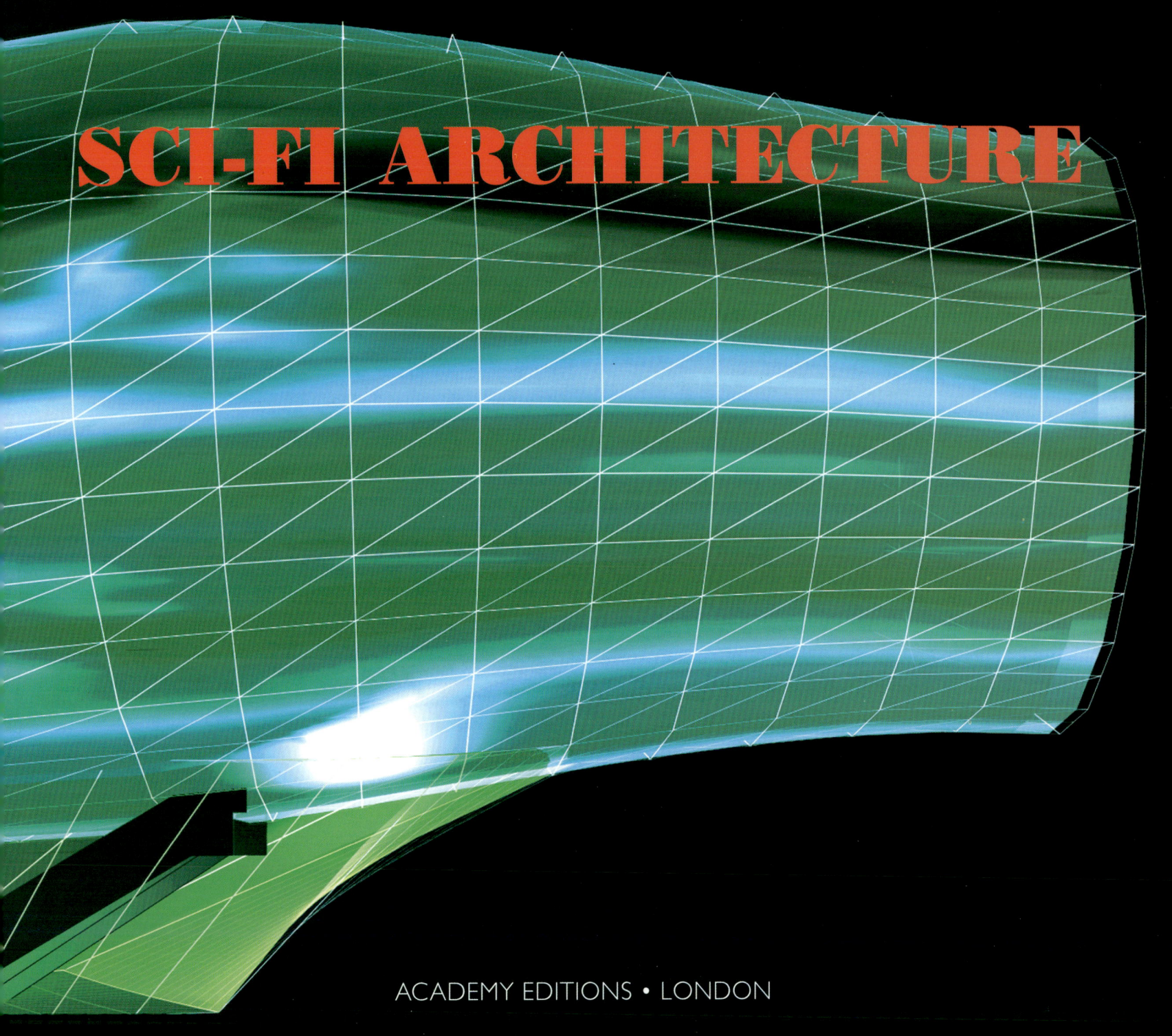

ACADEMY EDITIONS • LONDON

Acknowledgements

We would like to express our gratitude to all the contributors to *Architectural Design*.

All material is courtesy of the authors and architects unless otherwise stated. Attempts have been made to locate the sources of all images to obtain full reproduction rights, but in the very few cases where this process has failed to find the copyright holder, our apologies are offered. Photographic credits: *pp6* Tomio Ohashi; *pp34* Todd Dalland; *pp35 middle and below, 36-37* Durston Saylor; *pp48,50-53* Jörg Hempel; *pp54-55* David Loftus; *pp70-71* M Pillhoffer; *pp72-73* Christian Døgl, virtual real estate gesmbh; *pp1, 82-85* Yoshiharu Matsumura

Front and Back Cover: Kovac Malone, Queen Street Bar, Melbourne, 1998
bar/shelving detail
Inside Covers: Foreign Office Architects, Virtual House
Pages 2-3: Kovac Malone, Large Screen Cinema, inside view

EDITOR: Maggie Toy
EDITORIAL ASSISTANT: Bob Fear
PRODUCTION: Mariangela Palazzi-Williams
COPY EDITOR: Melissa Larner
DESIGN: Mario Bettella and Andrea Bettella/Artmedia

First published in Great Britain in 1999 by *Architectural Design*
42 LEINSTER GARDENS, LONDON W2 3AN

A division of John Wiley & Sons
Baffins Lane, Chichester, West Sussex PO19 1UD

ISBN: 0-471-98712-3

The Publishers and Editor do not hold themselves responsible for the opinions expressed by the writers of articles or letters in this magazine
Copyright of articles and illustrations may belong to individual writers or artists
Architectural Design Profile 138 is published as part of
Architectural Design Vol 69 3-4/1999
Architectural Design Magazine is published six times a year and is available by subscription

Printed and bound in Italy

Contents

EDITORIAL
MAGGIE TOY

One generation's ground-breaking science-fiction usually becomes the accepted norm of the next. Advances in materials and techniques over the century have eventually caused that which years ago was set firmly in the realms of the imagination to become reality.

Architects typically search other disciplines for inspiration and the worlds of science and science fiction are a popular source. For many architects, the dream is to achieve a living Utopia. Probably the first in this century to explore it was Antonio Sant'Elia (1888-1916), with his incredible drawings of stations and aerodromes, as well as new aerial cities with layered, terraced houses. Possibly the most famous utopian buildings are Le Corbusier's (1887-1965) Immeuble-villas and Ville Radieuse of 1922. Henri Sauvage (1873-1932) and Auguste Perret (1874-1954) made drawings for the ultimate community-living design, including enormous skyscrapers set amongst wide-open pedestrian spaces. All these were fantastic interpretations of a fiction in their day, but have since become real. Following the stage in which fiction becomes reality, there is frequently a third stage of critical derision.

The 1950s saw the designs for an optimistic future of Alison Smithson (1928-1993) and Peter Smithson (b1923), particularly in their House for the Future, devised for an exhibition in 1956. This design combined accepted aesthetics with carefully calculated ergonomic necessities and expectations of future lifestyle requirements.

In the 1960s, design was highly influenced by the space race. The idea that the conquest of outer space was within man's reach crystallised the sense of optimism and awe in a world seemingly able to harness highly refined technologies to realise peaceful ambitions on a heroic scale. Space-age styles soon became the currency of fashionable design and architecture. The designs of Oscar Neimeyer and Kisho Kurokawa clearly demonstrate this desire to reflect the aesthetics of the age. Archigram also emerged in the 60s, and carried right through the 70s their fictional solutions for our future lives. Ron Herron's Walking City of 1964 could still be used today as sketch designs for the latest sci-fi movies.

The development of 'high-tech' architecture as a style in the 1980s came from the interesting idea of using technological progress to inform and advance building. High-tech architecture became linked with a particular look and, like sci-fi architecture, concentrated more on the appearance of being projected into the future than the reality of it. The present era of futuristic design encompasses a desire to test materials and shapes as well as scientific theories. Frank Gehry's New Guggenheim Museum in Bilbao and the planned Victoria & Albert Museum Extension by Daniel Libeskind begin to give us a sense of future possibilities.

In this issue of *Architectural Design,* we feature aspects of the aesthetics and interpretation of science-fiction architecture, along with those designs that are attempting to bring science fiction into reality by the use of high technology.

The debate at the Royal Academy focuses on the nature of high-tech architecture and the fact that it is a design style rather than an accurate description. Clearly, as Iann Barron points out, architects are extremely behind in this area and have not managed to utilise the available resources, which would have considerably advanced the nature of our built environment. Rachel Armstrong directly addresses the science-fiction world, which conveys a highly integrated relationship between human, machine, artifice and nature in inner and outer space. Karin Damrau investigates a world in which boundaries are being continuously pushed – a world of invention that leads to progress. Through project presentations, FTL demonstrate the aesthetics of the future age as well as their process of extending the capacity of materials beyond the limits previously tested. Andrew Martin of FIN uses the space aesthetics of the 60s to design his inspirational restaurant interior in London. Reiser + Umemoto stretch the confines of architectural design, while Ben van Berkel and Caroline Bos demonstrate their ability to push the perameters of planning and architecture with their scheme for Arnhem's station complex. Foreign Office Architects declare their lack of interest in the future and their preference for the virtual, explaining that the notion of the future is static because it implies a conventional expectation of what that future will be, whilst the virtual is able to capture the dynamic nature of a situation.

As we move towards 2001, the year pinpointed by Stanley Kubrick in his film *2001, a Space Odyssey,* made in 1968, the styles of that space-obsessed era are being re-introduced. In much the same way that 1984 gave us an opportunity to assess the state's control over us, and to note that George Orwell's vision was not so far from the truth, the millennium is giving us the impetus to reassess the achievements of the century and look forward optimistically to the design style of the future.

OPPOSITE: Capsule House "K", Nagano, Japan, KIsho Kurokawa, 1973

FORUM

THE MYTH OF HIGH TECH
Royal Academy of Arts, London, June 1998

Paul Finch: The title of this afternoon's discussion: 'The Myth of High Tech', came out of a conversation between a small group of people who plan these events. Charles Jencks argued strongly that it should not be merely 'The Myth of High Tech', but 'The Myth and Beauty of High Tech', and I dare say the question of high tech as relating – how can I say this without the risk of getting eggs thrown at me immediately – in some senses to the Baroque, being about beautiful decoration independent of whatever else it may be, will arise during the course of the afternoon.

Robert Maxwell: Whether high tech is a style or not seems to depend on whether we view it from the inside or the outside. The insider sees it as a technique that responds directly to the needs of the client and puts no obstacle to their realisation. The outsider sees a series of obsessive artefacts that, in the words of the poet Robert Herrick, 'are too precise in every part'. Whatever else they do, they present the image of the machine, and that is to eliminate everything human except the immediate purpose. There are certain practical aspects of high-tech building that militate against this clarity. In the Pompidou Centre, for instance, the need to spray on fire protection results in a coarse structure. In order to restore the technical precision, it has to be further encased in aluminium or stainless steel tubing. This is neither cheap nor aesthetically consistent with the idea of exposing an underlying reality.

Paul Finch: Would anybody like to raise any point immediately following that, or pursue any issue with Bob before we move on?

Ian Ritchie: Just to add to that I think Bob's comments are appropriate to the Beaubourg, in the sense that the dream of this kind of future flexibility came face to face with the fire officer and that world of reality and actual public safety that the architect was supposedly serving.

Dalibor Vesely: May I make one little comment about flexibility? That dream was definitely cultivated to a certain point, but suddenly it was dropped. And yet the building as it stands at the moment is expected to be what I would call flexible. Now, we can push that aside, but I would ask, how flexible do we need it to be? If you go there, you see practically all the possible requirements in play. You see exhibitions coming and going. There's a floor with an information centre and a library. Nothing's changed there. They are quite content with the original layout. Some years ago one of our students undertook some research, and part of the research was the very question of exhibiting. The most flexible piece of the building, I have no doubt, is the temporary exhibition centre.

Robert Maxwell: The flexible 'shed' space, such as we see in the Sainsbury Centre at UEA and in an elongated vertical form at the Hong Kong and Shanghai Bank, is a form that is close to the classical. I've compared the design of the Sainsbury Centre at UEA with the Palazzo dei Congressi in a suburb of Rome to show that there are big similarities. I've always claimed that the shed leads back through history to... well, King's College Chapel is a shed, isn't it?

Peter Blundell Jones: But Foster is rather careless about the number of bays – that always seems to me to be the case. Stansted is presented as though it's an accident that it's square, that there are 11 bays each way, because it's supposed to be extendable. You're supposed to have as many bays as you like. No classical architect, least of all Mies, would be indifferent to that. Even his housing blocks look like prototypes – a kind of serial repetitive device that you could then run off the production line. That's the paradox with Mies. The ideology of flexibility and repetition was taken up by all his followers and was the great ideology of the 50s and 60s, and behind it is this monumentalist ideology stating that the buildings have to be finite, classical, and so transcendent they can't have anything to do with their function. They have to be completely clean.

Robert Maxwell: Well, the chapel at King's College is a sort of clean machine in that sense – pretty well empty.

Paul Finch: There's just one other point that I'd like raise before asking Colin Davies to speak, which is the extent to which the sort of buildings you spoke about are pushing technology, or are trying to do things with technology for which it's not quite ready. The first people to pursue these sorts of things always run up against certain practical difficulties. But by the time they're capable of being resolved, of course, you wouldn't be designing the same building in the same way anyway because things have moved on. Although it's a myth that you can't do it, actually it's not a myth in the sense that you *can* do it. You could do precisely those things that were being laid claim to.

Robert Maxwell: There was over-excitement about flexibility. It was exaggerated as an idea. It seemed as if architects could really treat their buildings as something that need not be an obstacle; then they would open up to all kinds of human futures. It was another 10 or 15 years before a survey of working spaces in London revealed that 99 per cent of all needs could be satisfied by a space 10 foot by 8 foot by 20 foot and that human bodies in fact always do exactly the same thing, such as stand up and sit down. And the flexibility that we thought was around the corner in 1972 didn't in fact arrive.

Paul Finch: I'm going to bring Colin in now.

Colin Davies: In my introduction to my book on high-tech architecture, I tried to point out its main characteristics: that its typical materials were metal and glass, that it adhered to a strict code of honesty in expression, that it usually embodied ideas about industrial production, that it used industries other than the building industry as sources both of technology and of imagery, and that it put a high priority on flexibility of use – what we've just been talking about. As far as I could see, high tech, as practised predominantly by UK architects Foster, Rogers and Grimshaw, lasted between 1967 and 1987; then it was all over – or, at least, it seemed like an exciting idea in 1988 that high tech might have come to and end and was possibly about to be superseded by something else. So I thought I'd write it as history.

Paul Finch: Actually, *Time* magazine has already listed the architects who made a difference. Norman Foster was the only British architect included, and, indeed, it was for the Hong Kong and Shanghai Bank.

It's quite interesting that Grimshaw's Eden project is both a hymn to nature and probably one of the most successful Lottery schemes, because it's doing something absolutely new, as opposed to accretial modernism which 'does up' the British Museum or 'does up' a power station. The question I wanted to ask you is whether you think that the high-tech architects have now used nature explicitly as a way, not simply of thinking about the design – taking biological models and so on and so forth – but of validating and justifying what they're doing?

Norman Foster says that his Reichstag project will be powered by a little power station that will take care of the local district. What is the fuel for this? Vegetable oil, which will be cropped in the fields nearby. So all of a sudden this project isn't simply about the restoration of one of the great symbolic buildings of the 20th century; it's all about rapeseed oil and sinking tubes 70 metres into the ground to cool them down. The main thing about this is that energy-wise it's just about as good as you can get.

Ian Ritchie: I'd just like to add something to that, having been at press conferences in Europe with the directors of Foster's where they put forward the case for the high-performance ecological skin to the building. It starts with the preconception: I like glass. How do I make it work? How do I make this entire building work? And it has been proven, not just at Commerz Bank but at other buildings, that having three or four levels of glass is absolute nonsense in terms of the cost in relation to the life of the building. There is again this desire for an image of a building. With certain architects that starts with glass in its totality: how can I make this thing work? What stories can I build into it that can, if you like, continue the myth?

Robert Maxwell: This myth of the image is demonstrated by the Sydney Opera House, which cost so much they had to invent the idea of a lottery in order to pay for it. When it was discovered that the structure couldn't stand up, an engineer had to find a way of resolving this, and when it was found that it didn't have the desired acoustic properties, a second building had to be built inside it. But that building generated enormous interest; its image made the architect famous and has become a source of new architecture. This demonstrates the power of image.

Architecture is becoming increasingly dumbed down – looking at it from the professional functionalist point of view – because now what catches is what goes. Any image that attracts the public generates entrance money. That's where the purely commercial values of global capitalism give you a situation that intellectuals mistake for, and call, 'the post-modern condition', where nothing is true except what sells.

Colin Davies: I believe that high tech went through the three usual phases: early phase, high phase and mannerist phase. It did become incredibly mannered, but something fundamental survived and was reapplied. It found a new job saving energy – just as illusory as the job it had dragging the building industry into the 20th century. It had to have a job to do. It always does. The discovery of green issues by Foster, Rogers and Grimshaw may be laughable, but certainly the market's right.

Dalibor Vesely: As an outsider, I find it interesting that the English are high-tech – very, very amusing indeed. When you come to this country the last thing you see is high-tech architecture being the dominating phenomenon in the UK. It is quite interesting to remember that when you read Prince Albert's speeches about the Great Exhibition, he says something like, 'the science and the knowledge can come from Germany, the art can come from France, and we're going to make and put it together'. So that's British high tech: the process.

David Turnbull: The questions of ecology and building performance become rather pathetic when they're considered solely in relation to the building rather than in relation to the larger territories or regions or organisations within the city. I've just been in Cairo, where the population is growing by one million people per year. The conditions of density in the city are quite extraordinary – sometimes 1,000 people per hectare – with very few high-rise buildings. These are incredible issues that really demand some kind of reflection on the condition of the city and on the status of technology in relation to that city.

Robert Maxwell: When we saw Colin Davies' slide of Lethaby's Brockhampton church, I had a strange feeling in my stomach. It's a beautiful church. If Lethaby was able to talk about construction and myth, which he did, it was because he was a very religious man. Arts and Crafts was essentially a religious movement, referring back to the wholeness of life under belief. If you think of the Pre-Raphaelites in England and the Nazarenes earlier on in Germany, those people really thought that there was a need to

regenerate society; that a Christian story, a Christian myth, would somehow remake society. That the high-tech people can use the idea of the Arts and Crafts Movement as a justification for their obsessive military machines offends me, frankly. It's an undue expenditure of money in a world where we have to think about the untold millions. I think that bringing up the city is another way of bringing up the relationship between architecture and culture. The high tech, as an expensive style, is good for a certain kind of images and therefore sales. That's all it's good for. It's not really architecture.

Paul Finch: I'm going to ask Andy Bow to say a few words as the apostolic representative of Sir Norman this afternoon.

Andy Bow: Rather than talking about the myth of the high tech, I'd like to offer some of my thoughts on the way technology is used within our office now, by referring to three different projects that I'm working on. Firstly, in terms of space – to use Nick Grimshaw's analogy of space, skin and structure – with world squares, the analysis of Trafalgar Square and Parliament Square, the very first thing we did was go to Bill Hillier's Unit at the Bartlet School of Architecture to understand the way in which people moved around all of these spaces that we've all come to know and love. Without this analysis it would have been impossible for us to even begin to contemplate how to deal with a master plan for that area. So straight away very advanced computer technologies for understanding the ways in which people moved through the city helped us in that process.

Secondly, the skin: at Albion Wharf, next to our office, there is a rising crescent. It's a mixed-use development. We have a facade that faces north, south, east and west, where we're trying to create glass balustrades that are 7 metres wide, and we have open-bowl glass that, with the flick of a switch, moves away.

And finally, in terms of structure, on the millennium footbridge, wind is an issue. There were many suggestions that we might begin to make glass balustrades, but they would be difficult to maintain and the structure would become three or four times as big. The solution that we've come up with is technology transfer – it's from motor racing: the air foil sections at the back of cars. So the balustrades are emerging as an air foil in section. Now, for me it's quite natural to learn from technology transfer. I have daily conversations with Norman Foster, and our conversations are about philosophy, humanity, scale, rhythm, colour, texture. The conversations every day of the week are not about nuts and bolts like facades, and I think that it's very important to say that. Technology in our office is the servant of the concept. You're only as good as the last idea that you drew; the pencil is everything, and it's as basic as that. I feel uncomfortable with accusations of being liars. Problems evolve, and we try to find the right solutions, and ultimately we're in search of the most beautiful solution. That's really the stage that we're at now.

Paul Finch: And now we're going to hear from Ram Ahronov, who worked for six years as a project architect at Richard Rogers' and then was an associate at Foster and Partners.

Ram Ahronov: I thought I'd pick up on the role of visual art, which, I think, is a very important aspect of the aesthetics and meaning of what we call 'high tech'. Take Stansted Airport, whose roof is almost the area of two football pitches. One of the big problems was what to do with the rainwater. Either you

channel it through the diagonal or through the gutter. Now, neither of these fairly conventional solutions was suitable for this particular case. The solution that we were able to find after about three years' research was from Finland. There, they've developed a UV system that allows you to take the rainwater pipe horizontally by using a siphon system. You see a kind of flexible covered pipe and inside the building a panel system that covers the whole ceiling of the terminal. This gave us two elements: on the one hand we could take all the water horizontally – you see nothing at all on the building – on the other, the pipe can be exposed once you take off the panel, so for maintenance and repair it's always open. We brought those ideas together, but the major concept was the aesthetic aspect.

Paul Finch: I think we'll move straight on to Chris McCarthy, who is an engineer, formerly with Ove Arup and now with the thriving and ever-expanding practice of Battle McCarthy. They're best known for their advanced work on extreme energy-saving systems and the use of nature as part of building structures and services.

Chris McCarthy: I was taken to Mippin at the beginning of the year – that's where you end up with 10,000 planners and surveyors – and they were all debating the 'big deal'. It suddenly occurred to me that it was all about looking at cities as 'the deal', and the way that transactions relating to our urban environment, and all our architectural decisions now are taken very quickly. One of the developers came over to me. I was talking about the work I've done, and he said, 'Oh, yes, that was great stuff, but that was just about space and throwing the services and structure outside the building to get maximum space'. It was depressing that here were the people making 90 per cent of the decisions about the future of architecture, and structure, quality of space and energy weren't on the agenda.

Shortly afterwards, I went to a conference on land-fill sites, which I thought was quite similar. They were talking about waste management of the material, something called 'site fabrication'. These are the real issues, and these are the people who are going to make the decisions about the future of technology, not architects. They went on to say that the *biggest* issue affecting land-fill sites, building construction and reduction of waste is adaptability; not flexibility but adaptability. Why are you building car parks that you can't adapt in the future into homes?

What I'm going to be talking about is the engineer as a kind of high priest of technology. What is the role of the engineer? You could say that architects are about applied art and we're about applied science. As applied scientists, our agenda, our brief, is to maximise use of materials, energy and skills to the benefit of mankind. The other issue that we're faced with as structural engineers is the role of myth; we were trying to do things that were unnaturally real. At the same time we were becoming aware that the structures we were creating were bigger than they needed to be, and there was more energy associated with those.

Taking a step back, if there is a need to close one door in architecture, you can open another, ie close the door of the 'high tech' and open the door of the 'new tech'. It's really going to be 'energy tech'. From working with architects on different projects, I've discovered that you are great space planners. As a structural engineer I've been rediscovering the atom. Moving into the area of nano-technology and separating atoms is also all about space. You can't cram them in. You've got to come up with three-dimensional space relations between atoms.

Bernard Tschumi Architects, Performance Hall and Exhibition Centre, Rouen, France

The actual technology is so much simpler to understand than a building, ie understanding how these different molecules compare. This is the sort of thing architecture should be moving into: starting to think about the relationship between molecules, and expanding that out to a cornice. Or, conversely, you can say, 'This is a performance delight. I want this to do this; I want that to do that', which is then involving industry in the conversation. If you go to ICI, where they've been doing all this work, they call it architecture, but they've never had an architect visit them.

I think the role of the architect and of the engineer in the field of nano-technology, atomic technology or genetic engineering is going to become part of our field. It does exist. We've been involved in designing composite footbridges and plastic footbridges for Lisbon. We understand that there is a need. There is a value in this technology transfer from a conventional steel bridge to the new technology. The bit that isn't so clear is the area where, for example, we did the review for Greenpeace on the Dome. Should it be PTFE or should it be PVC? It's a very unnerving and risky subject. Where is the architect? We're now saying these new materials are going to be created; we must debate them openly with people like Greenpeace. We must look at these materials and see if there is a future for them. If in the future we need to close the door so that high tech can go forward, I think the appeal of genetic engineering should open the debate. This is something that should be discussed openly amongst architects, because it will lead you into the issue of the plastic pipe that Ram specified earlier.

Paul Finch: The idea that the architect should know about molecules just when the schools of architecture thought they could knock a year off the course is going to mean that they'll have to put two or three on!

Ian Ritchie: Picking up on Chris' point about molecules, I think what's interesting for an architect interested in duct industry and the nano aspects of it, is that it requires finance from industry. Industry won't finance it because it has its own little secret research programmes. An architect is a very humble little being, and the market-place for building materials, as seen by the big industrialists, is actually fairly insignificant. Therefore, the ability of architects to have a signficant influence raises fundamental questions about one's ability to actually do something about it.

Chris McCarthy: I feel that the architect's conversation is very much about the final product. There is a question, a moral issue, that concerns the Dome. If you use, say, a PVC-membrane roof, you're upsetting the Green Party, and if you investigate the basis of their argument, it's not founded. The greatest thing the high-tech engineers can do for architects – and I've always done this – is to give them a vision of the future. I think you're in the business of looking at what you've done and what you're going to do and how that will affect the future. The scientists that I work with don't see beyond their lab. They work in a test-tube. Certain people just can't see tomorrow. I think the great success of high tech was in communicating technology to the public.

Robert Maxwell: But I think you're far too optimiotic to think that architects are anywhere near taking on what you've defined.

Paul Finch: It's a bit like the battle over whether steel or concrete can produce the most economical or strongest bridge.

Alan Jones: I don't think it's necessarily true that high tech means new materials. Many of the examples we saw earlier actually used old materials in new ways, and that, in some ways, can be seen as high tech as well. The way that it becomes high tech, if that's the right expression, is through the integration of thought that we're talking about now. By bringing those thought processes together and by the transfer of technology you produce something that is new, that is different, that has a style of its own. I'm not sure whether the Dome is actually high tech. It uses materials that are established; it doesn't use them in a particularly different way. Other examples take materials and use them in different ways. The Eden project was not built because it was looking for somewhere to go: it's in the right place at the right time. It's in Cornwall; it's in a quarry because that provides the right sort of climate to do what they want to do within that building; it's in a very sheltered location.

Paul Finch: Iann Barron has an extraordinary CV, which I commend to you all if you haven't already read it. He designed his first computer when he was still at Cambridge and was running the first mini-computer company in the UK in the mid-60s. I suppose we shouldn't be too surprised that at the moment he's involved with a virtual reality company called the Vision Group, which, as I understand it, supplies programmes or software – 'kit', to use the loosest term. The company is also involved in what might loosely be called the design of that kit.

Iann Barron: I must say that I speak to you with more than my normal diffidence. I too, am an architect, but I'm a computer architect. I don't think that I work in a different way from any other architect: I have a problem; I have a lot of issues, and I synthesise them. Actually – and this is the point that I want to make – I think that good scientists, good technologists, use exactly the same processes as architects. We choose beautiful solutions. It may not be obvious to anybody outside. Sometimes beauty is in the eye of the architect anyway. I don't think there is that gulf between one profession and another. We're really trying to do the same sort of thing; it's just that our problem area concerns different materials. I sympathise with all of you. I have a hell of a lot of problems designing things.

Dalibor Vesely: What's also interesting is that science, if you follow its development in the last few decades, goes from physics to something like polymers, for instance. Nowadays it's almost impossible to say whether you're in physics or biology. Some decades ago, it was clear-cut. What I'm really saying is that science itself moves from, say, physics – from physical structures – to biological structures and eventually, probably, to certain kinds of human structures. You are, in one sense, almost moving into psychiatry. About seven years before he died, Louis Kahn received a letter from NASA asking him to come down to Houston. He replied saying, 'I'm sorry, you've probably got the wrong person; it's not me'. They said, 'No, we know exactly who we want; we want you'. They wanted him to work with the people designing the interior of the capsule. They especially wanted him because, they said, 'We've been working on it for a number of years and we're now convinced that we're not getting anywhere, and you may be able to help', which he did. I remember when I finished engineering my teachers said, 'When you go up the stairs to architecture, don't forget. The architect will be moving towards engineering', and we didn't believe them.

Andy Bow: Ten years ago I hadn't designed a building with inflatable structures; I have now. I worked on a 200-metre-long wind canopy in Plymouth with Peter Rice. I hadn't worked on membrane structures before. I'm quite convinced that those of us who are spared the next ten years and who assemble in this room in a decade's time will see that the whole thing has moved on again. I'm absolutely convinced of that fact. I think it's enormously exciting. The gap between architecture and engineering is minuscule. We're very lucky in London, because the best engineers in the world are here.

Ian Ritchie: I was interested in Iann Barron's reference to the real world of building as being somewhat bespoke, as against the Ford analogy. I remember Geoffrey Broadbent saying that the nearest thing an architect could deal with in terms of, let's say, computer architecture is to print a silicon chip on a bigger scale on a bit of glass from which to make a balustrade. There's a relationship between that flow of information and a couple of things that come together, which are the virtual world and the real world. More and more, as architects work all day in front of screens, there's a desensitising of the humanity. I know that from experience, having worked on 3-D computers for the last 15 years (and not Apple Macs) and having extreme difficulty training people on them, getting information distributed and knowing where the difficulties are – it's a virtual world. It's tasteless, untouchable, non-smelly. It's a very strong illusion. It's also an extremely strong architecture that is real. It exists in the minds of all these people who invent it. One can take the analogy that I think Martin Pawley once made: 'He said, "You're going to live in a virtual world", and I asked him, "And where am I going to piss?"' But 50 per cent, certainly, of my life is in this virtual world. A translation of that into the real one, which I think Chris was moving into, is that there is through that technology a fluid and natural, rather than a mechanical Victorian, idea, which one sees in high tech, that will emerge in future architecture. That, I feel, is certain.

Robert Maxwell: I do agree with that, and I would just like to say that I hope the fact that I proposed the demise of the high tech doesn't lead you to think that I'm against progress. Of course, we can't avoid progress; it's inevitable. People will always look for quicker, neater, cheaper and more effective ways of doing things, so I don't want to stop science. In attacking the high tech I was not attacking the march of science, but I do see, at the same time, that as science uncovers for us a more and more complex universe – nature – the question of what kind of human structure we can fit to that, which will hold social coherence, becomes more and more crucial. In classical architecture, for instance, decoration was derived from a metaphor for structure, and all the parts of that decoration fitted together in an ordered hierarchy. Nature has become so complex for us, and we're so aware of this, that we no longer have an image of the whole. So, my interest in the high tech has been increased here because I see it as a rather naïve, a rather rough-and-ready, a rather Victorian way of trying to come to terms with the future. In terms of the perspective that you've raised here, it actually becomes fetchingly whimsical and human because it's concerned with the problems of every day. I really was touched by Ram's account of the rainwater pipe, which is a superb piece of design in itself. There is a very, very long distance from understanding the complexity of nature and decoding it, and being able to create on our side a complexity that is deeply human.

Paul Finch: It's an impossible afternoon to sum up, not least because there's a whole series of other things that we might have talked about with more time. If Charles Jencks had been here he would have had plenty to say about decoration and his view that, say in the work of Eva Jiricna or some aspects of Richard Rogers', this is our equivalent of the Baroque at its highest. We didn't talk much about the divorce between high-tech architecture and the idea of technology and replication or repeatability, except for the point about buildings being bespoke. There's a notion that high-tech buildings cannot deliver their promise of cheapness and affordability because they never replicate. That's why they're such expensive prototypes in the first place.

I'd like to end with – I think we touched on it very briefly – what for me is a very interesting building that relates to a whole series of the arguments and conversations this afternoon: Frank Gehry's new Guggenheim Museum in Bilbao. As regards the relationship between high tech and the Arts and Crafts, here is a building in which every single titanium panel has come out of a standardised process and yet each one is different; each is pre-formed to go onto a specific point on the structure. As a result of the miracle of computer technology, the design information can go down wires, the jigs can be set without human intervention, and what you get are things that in other industries are becoming bespoke and standard at the same time, such as the Nike trainer where your foot has been digitalised and your trainer is just slightly different from the next one coming off the line; and it doesn't really cost you that much more, if any more at all. The relationship between the standardised and the customised starts to vanish, and at this point the idea of the hand-crafted and the machine-crafted start to converge. Arts and Crafts meets the vision of technology, prefabrication and standardisation in a new way.

The outcome, as it happens, goes right back to Iann's earlier point. Here is the building that has become *the* architectural image of this year and possibly this decade. Why so? It's partly to do with the fact that it looks so different. It has shades of Sydney Opera House, but this is Sydney Opera House with a bit of chaos thrown into the structure and, of course, with the most expensive metal (until palladium recently overtook it), titanium, used to an extravagant extent – millimetres thick on the outside. It has been photographed; it has become advertising architecture. Now, how does the client respond to that? In an interesting way. The museum has registered the architecture and, as a consequence, the artefact – not what's inside, but the building itself – as an artwork. It now has copyright. If you want to go and take a photograph of that building, which you then sell for profit, you'll be breaking copyright law, and they can sue you.

This is a coming together of Arts and Crafts, high tech and standardisation. Yet going back to what it is that we've created, we've created an artistic image which is, I think, a metaphor for what we've been discussing.

IANN BARRON
A REAL HIGH-TECHNOLOGIST

I am a high-technologist. I am an architect, but I'm a computer architect. My skill is designing mazes for electrons to run around. The first computer I designed would have just about fitted into this room. The second was probably about the size of this table. The third was known as a twin-tub washing machine – that sizes it fairly accurately. The fourth was the size of a hi-fi unit. The last would fit into the palm of your hand. And, of course, the power of that last computer was many millions of times greater than the one that would scarcely fit into this room 20 years earlier.

I've also run parallel to the scene of high-tech architecture because I've had the pleasure of being the patron for buildings designed by Michael Hopkins, Norman Foster, Richard Rogers and, most recently, Chris Wilkinson. In this respect, I'm a client who knows about high-tech buildings.

Of course, to me the irony of high-tech buildings is that, whatever they are, they certainly are not high-tech in the sense that I would understand. If I want to look for high-tech design, I don't look to the building industry or architecture these days. If I want to look at materials, I look to the aerospace industry or space. If I want to look at design techniques, I look, again, to the aerospace industry or the car industry, because those are the places where the fundamentals of design are being forged; in applications that can afford the high cost of development and where the volume is great enough to achieve a level of detail impossible in bespoke architecture.

The one area where it does seem that high-tech architecture has been high tech in the real sense is in terms of structure. The interesting thing about all high-tech buildings is that they manifest as great a development as that which occurred during the Gothic period in the ability to conceive, design and build in new ways ever more intricate and delicate structures.

I'm somewhat amused that many people are offended by the use of high tech as an aesthetic. Why should the appropriate use of technology, which to me is the best form of architecture, not be expressed directly in the exterior design, the visible parts of the building? It's important to persevere with high tech; you've got to continue using the technologies that are becoming available to create better buildings, and go on exploiting the aesthetics that those new techniques and new technologies create. That is the way to achieve great architecture in the future.

I'd like to look at what might perhaps be the technologies that will affect the aesthetics of buildings in the future. The obvious one is information technology, which clearly affects the way in which people wish to use buildings, the mode of transit between them, and the use and operation within.

The second aspect is the use of wireless facilities. The idea that one can communicate and control remotely without physical connections between two elements is emerging everywhere and this is influencing events inside the building. In 10 to 20 years, we can expect all control and communication within a building to be without wires, which gives one a great deal of flexibility and eliminates many internal design problems.

The third area is nano-technology. In the past, we've been able to make things on a human scale. The watch, so small and detailed, was a miracle of ingenuity. We've also been able to make things that are larger than human scale, to amplify our muscles: cranes, diggers and so forth. But we've had very little skill in creating structures that are significantly smaller than human scale. What semi-conductive technology has shown is that we will be able to create techniques that can fabricate things a thousand times smaller than anything we might reasonably envisage today. We will make motors, mechanical devices, cooling devices, moving devices that are one-hundredth of a millimetre across – dust size. This will significantly affect the way in which we design in the future.

There's an apocryphal story about a conversation between Bill Gates and the chairman of General Motors: Bill said, 'Well, if you assumed technology curves like I do, you'd be making cars that went at 500 miles an hour, and you'd be selling them for 10 cents'. And the chairman of GM looked at him and said, 'Yeah, and they'd be crashing every four hours, and what would I be doing for my customers?' I make no apologies for computers; they are appalling. I am distressed by the facilities that surround us, which are based on the way computers were 30 years ago. When I designed computers and delivered them in 1970, they were expected to run perfectly without error. Now, most systems crash every day. However, computer programmes are becoming much more complex and people are automatically building-in and comparing different routes. Computers are evolving into something more resilient that is much closer to the way in which the human brain works – not by design, but by trial and error. So things are going to improve.

I was one of the early prophets of the micro-processor. It seemed to me that it was going to make a radical change to the world in which we lived. I wasn't very clear how; I just knew that technology creates markets, creates the future. When I talked about my proposals I used to use the example of electric motors. I would say, 'How many electric motors do you have in your house?' People would pause; they would think; they would say, 'two', 'three', 'four'. The answer, of course, is probably 50 or 100. They are hidden in all sorts of places and used in some improbably elaborate ways. My favourite example was an electric knife or razor. I predicted that the same thing would happen with micro-processors. And sure enough, you can use a micro-processor to replace a spring in a car, creating an active suspension system that adjusts the height, ride and movement of the car by computation and not by mechanical force. Nano-technology is exactly the same. I've no idea what it's going to be used for, but, boy, it's going to be significant!

The next area I would like to emphasise is decoration. What has happened over the centuries is that architecture has lost micro-decoration. Gothic or Rococo buildings were covered in decoration. We've got rid of it all by trying to simplify and reduce cost and labour. The increasing ability of computers to fabricate decorative patterns and details, each one different from the next, will change all this.

The last area I'd like to discuss is the design tools themselves. When I look at products, I don't see them, perhaps, in the same way that architects do. I see the design technology behind them. I'm always struck by the way in which innovation and art come out of an underlying technology. One of my favourite examples from the past is the mini-skirt. Nearly ten years before the mini-skirt became fashionable, someone invented the twin-lock knitting machine, which made stockings that laddered far less frequently. This led to tights, and with tights came the mini-skirt.

If I look at a modern popular design icon, such as the Ford car I see two things: I see virtual reality, and I see nerves. That car looks good whichever direction you look at it from, and wherever the light falls on it as you move around it. It has very good specular properties. That's because designers were able to look at it in three dimensions even at the prototype stage. And why nerves? 'Nerves' are a non-uniform, round, binary supply: a way of defining a three-dimensional curve, which again is a very useful design tool. Look at that car's beautiful three-dimensional curves! The same kind of technology is going to become available to architects because of the reducing cost of computers. As a result, architects will have the ability to visualise their designs much more effectively. Furthermore, we now have the tools to create flexible, curved, beautiful structures.

Raybould House, KOLATAN/MACDONALD STUDIO

COLIN DAVIES
HINDSIGHT OR FORESIGHT?

In the introduction to my book *High-Tech Architecture*, published by Thames and Hudson in 1988, I tried to point out the main characteristics of high-tech architecture: that its typical materials were metal and glass; that it adhered to a strict code of honesty in expression; that it usually embodied ideas about industrial production; that it used industries other than the building industry as sources both of technology and of imagery, and that it put a high priority on flexibility of use. It seemed to me at the time – 10 years ago – that high tech was a characteristically British style (I certainly wasn't the first person to point that out), and I suggested that it could be applied to practically anything designed by Norman Foster, Richard Rogers, Nicholas Grimshaw or Michael Hopkins between 1967 and 1987. Note the dates; note the past tense. As far as I could see, high tech was all over – at least, it seemed like an exciting idea in 1988 that high tech might be over and was possibly about to be superseded by something else. So I thought I'd write it as history.

It had begun in 1967 with the Reliance Controls Factory, the last building to be designed by Foster and Rogers as a partnership, and it had come to an end in 1987 with those two great urban buildings of the late 80s, the Hong Kong and Shanghai Bank and the Lloyds Building. Of course, its impetus had been kept going in the 70s by the Pompidou Centre. So I said, it's finished – come to an end. Unaccountably, the architects concerned failed to notice that high tech had passed into history, and they continued blithely designing buildings that any reasonable person would have to admit conformed to all the main defining characteristics of high tech. There were many buildings by Grimshaw. He was the one who stayed most steadfastly faithful to the cause, with Waterloo, the Western Morning News, the RAC Control Centre, the British Pavilion at Seville and so on. There were all those airports: Stansted, Che Lap Kok and Terminal Five, all of them reasonably described as high tech. There was the Century Tower by Foster, the Channel Four building by Rogers, the European Court of Human Rights, the Media Centre at Lords' cricket ground, about to be finished by Future Systems and, of course, the Millennium Dome. They're all high tech. OK, I was wrong. It didn't come to an end. It's alive and well, so I suppose I'm going to have to defend it as required.

There is a certain irony that now I should be called upon to defend it against the accusation that it is myth, that it is, in Robert Maxwell's words, 'an elaborate artifice'. It's difficult too, because in a sense, yes, I agree. The only difference is I don't see why this is a problem. Yes, there is a mythical – actually, I prefer the word 'fictional' – dimension to high tech, but then that's what makes it architecture. It doesn't just solve practical problems in economical ways, like oil rigs, ships or aeroplanes, or the space vehicles that parts of it sometimes superficially resemble; it carries meaning, and it strives for beauty.

But beneath the fiction, beneath all the symbolism and image-making, all those external-tension steel structures and exposed services ducts, which, as Robert Maxwell points out, are almost never justifiable in practical building terms, there is always, nevertheless, a more important underlying philosophy. And this is what Bob has failed to recognise or to acknowledge – high tech's more fundamental virtues. If I had to choose one word to sum these up, that word would be 'unity', the unity of process and product, of designing and making, of architecture and construction.

You could argue – I think it has been argued before – that the historical roots of the high-tech style are not to be found in the picturesque landscape tradition of the 18th century, as Bob suggests, or even in 19th-century engineering structures, but in the Arts and Crafts Movement: in the hand-made furnishings of William Morris, the folksy vernacular houses of Philip Webb, Ernest Gimpson or WR Lethaby (Brockhampton Church, for example: a thatched roof on a concrete deck).

This apparent paradox that high tech and Arts and Crafts have something fundamentally in common deserves further discussion elsewhere. In the meantime, let me just offer this quote from Norman Foster's AIA Gold Medal acceptance speech:

> Originally people didn't put thatched roofs on cottages to create a homely folksy effect; they were using thatch for its weatherproofing and insulating qualities and because it was the material to hand. The materials to hand now do not necessarily come from a nearby field, but the way we develop a concept as a direct response to needs – of people, client, ecology and so on – has the potential to create a new vernacular that is the equivalent of the thatched cottage.

So here we have Sir Norman Foster appreciating the qualities of low-tech thatched cottages and using words like 'vernacular'. It seems strange. It may be true that architects like Foster are interested in technology in the broad sense, and that their architecture symbolises faith in the progress of science and technology. But they're interested in technology as architects and builders, not as scientists and philosophers. Put more simply, they're interested in construction, and this interest is becoming increasingly rare among architects, which is why I want to argue that high tech is becoming increasingly important. High-tech architects are interested in the processes of building, especially the industrialised processes, and in the ways that construction and architecture can be unified.

It was already clear ten years ago that real high technologies, that is, digital and biological technologies, were leaving high tech far behind. There may have been an architectural equivalent of the oil rig or the space vehicle, but it wasn't at all clear how there could be an architectural equivalent of the silicon chip. Of course, since then, avant-garde architects have struggled to find that equivalent, to find some way in which architecture can participate in the digital/biological revolution. We have architecture as network, as organism, as landscape, as ecological system, architecture that imitates the emergent forms of nature on the one hand and of cyberspace on the other. And, of course, much of this architecture exists only in cyberspace. It's an architecture of the mind, not of the body. The tendency is towards a separation of mind and body, of idea and substance, of the imagined and the real, of the virtual and the actual – in other words, between architecture and construction. Even the everyday application of digital technology in design, such as computer analysis and visualisation of structural forces (Daniel Libeskind's Victoria and Albert Museum extension, for example, with the stresses in the structure visualised by computer) tends to widen this gap between architecture and construction. The extension finds its way from the imagination to reality by means of computer analysis, but this is no kind of unity; this is just a perpetuation of the old divide that has existed since the Renaissance: the architect, trained as painter, sculptor, philosopher, imagines the form, and the engineer or builder makes it stand up. High-tech architects don't do this – or at least they try not to do it. They strive to close the gap between architect and builder, and that's what I find admirable about them.

A high-tech architect's response to the new biological, digital paradigm can be found in Nick Grimshaw's Eden project in Cornwall. It's interesting how the story has changed. The fiction is no longer the mechanical but the biological. It doesn't look anything like a machine; it looks like a honeycomb or a cluster of cells or frogspawn – something organic. But the point is it isn't just an image; it is also a very clever piece of construction, and to that extent it is still within the high-tech fold. Cyberspace is fun, and it has a kind of architecture, but it doesn't have much to do with building or, for that matter, space as it is experienced and used by the human body. Cyberspace hasn't abolished the primary conditions of a building's existence; they still apply. The earth, the sky, gravity and climate, form and space, the qualities of materials – these are the guiding principles of high tech.

So perhaps I dismissed all those external steel structures and that exposed ductwork too lightly. What are they but the primary conditions of the building's existence made into architecture through technology? The external ducts may now have turned into sunshades, which do a similar job, but the point is, they're visible; they're part of the architecture; they're not excluded.

Gravity and climate are not dismissed as a boring nuisance, a mere impediment to the imagination, as they are by certain deconstructivists or painters turned architects; they are used to make the architecture.

Let's look at something more recent: the Commerz Bank in Frankfurt, also by Norman Foster, completed last year. I don't know if this counts as high tech any more. Probably not. But in it we see a similar kind of spatial inventiveness, the same struggle to make an architecture out of the forces of gravity and climate. It is a naturally ventilated skyscraper. It has internal gardens that step up the building like a giant staircase, and they're planted not with palm trees and other displaced tropical species but with maples and cypresses and hundred-year-old olive trees, living and breathing naturally in the fresh, unconditioned air. It's a pretty extraordinary experience, the interior of this building. Tony Hunt has pointed out to me that the structure of this skyscraper, with its composite steel-and-concrete columns and its multi-storey frames, is actually much more sophisticated than that of the Hong Kong and Shanghai Bank. Certainly, it has a conceptual elegance. Chris Wise, who is the designer of this structure, tells me that all its components were scheduled on a single side of A4 paper – amazing conceptual elegance.

So why is it that I find this bank, less satisfying architecturally than the Hong Kong and Shanghai? Perhaps it's because in the 10 years since the completion of the Hong Kong Bank the gap between architecture and construction has widened. Architects have been pushed closer towards the margins of the productive building industry. Many details of the bank were dictated not by Norman Foster and his colleagues but by the client's own engineers, project managers and sub-contractors. That gap that has opened up is clearly perceptible in the finished building. Its unity has been compromised. Amongst other things, its beautifully simple and elegant structure doesn't breathe.

Architectural magazine editors, like Paul Finch of the *Architect's Journal,* are probably already preparing their millennium editions and compiling lists of the century's top 10 buildings. I don't think Commerz Bank will come close, but the Hong Kong and Shanghai Bank, the great masterpiece of the high-tech style, despite all its flaws and follies, will be right up there at the top.

ROBERT MAXWELL
INSIDE OUT?

Whether or not we see high tech as a style seems to depend on whether we see it from the inside or the outside. Insiders – proponents of what we call high-tech style – see it as a technique that goes directly to the needs of the client. They don't think it's about style; they think it's about what's real. An image of the machine is therefore presented, eliminating everything human except the building's immediate purpose. The outsider, however, may see it as a series of obsessive artefacts that, in the words of the poet Robert Herrick, 'are too precise in every part'.

The basis of the high-tech appeal is that science and technology are demonstrated to be making the future. With high tech you have the force behind you; no one will ever think that you're a fuddy duddy, and, if you do it right, it will be a beautiful building. Nick Grimshaw has insisted that his architecture is about the artefact; putting materials together with respect, even love. He wants to be a sort of latterday follower of Ruskin. Norman Foster insists that his concerns are to do with people: the architect should be primarily an enabler. Richard Rogers, in explaining the Pompidou Centre back in 1972, insisted that it was all about change and adaptability.

As image, this is the final version of the modern style, the culmination of the machine aesthetic. It was not intended to be a style but it became one because it produced artefacts of a consistent character, and this consistency, in the end, filled a space that had to be named. It represents the last stage of architecture, stripped down to essentials. Grimshaw has named those essentials: structure, space, skin. All this may not be the result of following a style, but it must be the result of something invariable – an invariable attitude I suppose. This attitude is best characterised as belief in naturalism. What we perceive as a high-tech style is a consequence of believing that the building can be completely transparent to life so that it reveals life as it is – or, at least, as it wants to be, for there is an idealism at work here. Functionalism is not to be an 'ism' but something that really liberates from convention.

Ideal structures are the hull of a rowing boat or the glider, where concentration on the physical performance of minimal materials under stress produces a naked structure that appears to owe everything to science and nothing to culture. Science deals with the forces of nature, and so should architecture. The shell represents an ideal that is an acute combination of structure, skin and living space, and the architect of the shell is nature. This is a philosophy of design that emanated from Dorothy Thompson's seminal book, *On Growth and Form*, of 1914. In the act of building, the structure provides a basic framework, and both symbolises and *is* necessity. High-tech buildings expose their structure as the essential aspect of their nature, and in doing so they also celebrate structure as an aspect of truth. Exposing the surfaces on the outside is a further way of revealing the truth.

But there are certain practical aspects of building that militate against this clarity. In the Pompidou Centre, for instance, the need to spray on fire protection results in a coarse structure. To restore the technical precision, it has to be further encased in aluminium or stainless-steel tubing. This is neither cheap nor aesthetically consistent with the idea of exposing an underlying reality. It's not a stripping down but a building up. The structure you see is an elegant sheathing more monumental than the real structure it protects. So a sophisticated high-tech building is not the direct result of practical necessity but an elaborate artifice that speaks, often eloquently, of a necessity that has been invented. The reason why the Pompidou has so much structure is that the architects wanted it to have large floor spaces uninterrupted by columns in the name of flexibility. Every single beam had to be a deep lattice girder, a form usually adopted for engineering structures like bridges. A column-free floor would indeed be very useful if the intention were to install an ice-hockey rink or dodgem cars. So far, such uses have not proved necessary for the Pompidou to function as a library and art gallery. So in the interest of possibilities the structure has been inflated, making it heroic in scale. Structure and space are combined in such a way as to declare an ideological commitment, and the monumental returns as a privileged category.

This doesn't arise out of any inadequacy on the part of the architect but out of a desire – a desire to reach out to the future and be ready. It's precisely this desire that lifts a building into the realm of rhetoric and sustains its mythic aspect. People have responded to this in due measure, and it has been immensely popular, thereby justifying an expense far beyond what strict cost-accounting would have allowed. Thus for function to exist as myth it has to be made larger than life and given the strangeness of the shape of things to come. It points to a mythic future, beckons to utopia. This is the myth of the high tech. At the same time, it has a familiar aspect. It has become a popular myth. Because it speaks in the name of truth to nature, it appears to be free from artistic intent or personal whim. It appears as an objective style independent of personal expression, the result of engineering science, the way oil refineries and power stations are free from expression. Given our native puritanism, our ambiguity about treating the architect as an artist at all, does this not explain why the high-tech style has been such a potent factor in British architecture? It represents a group value not a personal vision. The corridors of power are still comforting themselves with the assumption that architecture resembling engineering is less likely to conceal a personal vision.

But far from pursuing purely functional requirements, the high tech projects a highly ideological belief in the power of science and technology as the only sure way of anticipating the future and achieving power. Far from being matter of fact and realistic in its approach, it reflects an underlying romanticism about life and living in the tradition of English landscape architecture, which looks natural but is, in fact, highly artificial. On this reading, it's not so odd that some such style should surface in Britain rather than, say, the United States, where landscape simply imitates the wilderness or rejects it. Here, the wilderness must be civilised and absorbed into culture as an amenity, yet made to look as if it happened naturally. The stroll around the park is agreeable and no threat to young ladies; but it skirts the temple of love or the grotto. This flirtation with what I call 'sweet disorder' can be taken to represent a continuity in the British pursuit of happiness: no art please, we're British.

It's true that exponents of the high-tech approach have been changing along with everything else. It seems that change is hardly something the architect must strive to accommodate, but something that overtakes us. As the century rolls to a close, Nick Grimshaw is happy to disclose that his clients are demanding something else:

Clients have come to perceive that what is justified in the name of order, economy and geometry is governed also by other forces. We now have clients who expect architecture to be an art and to have creative force behind it.

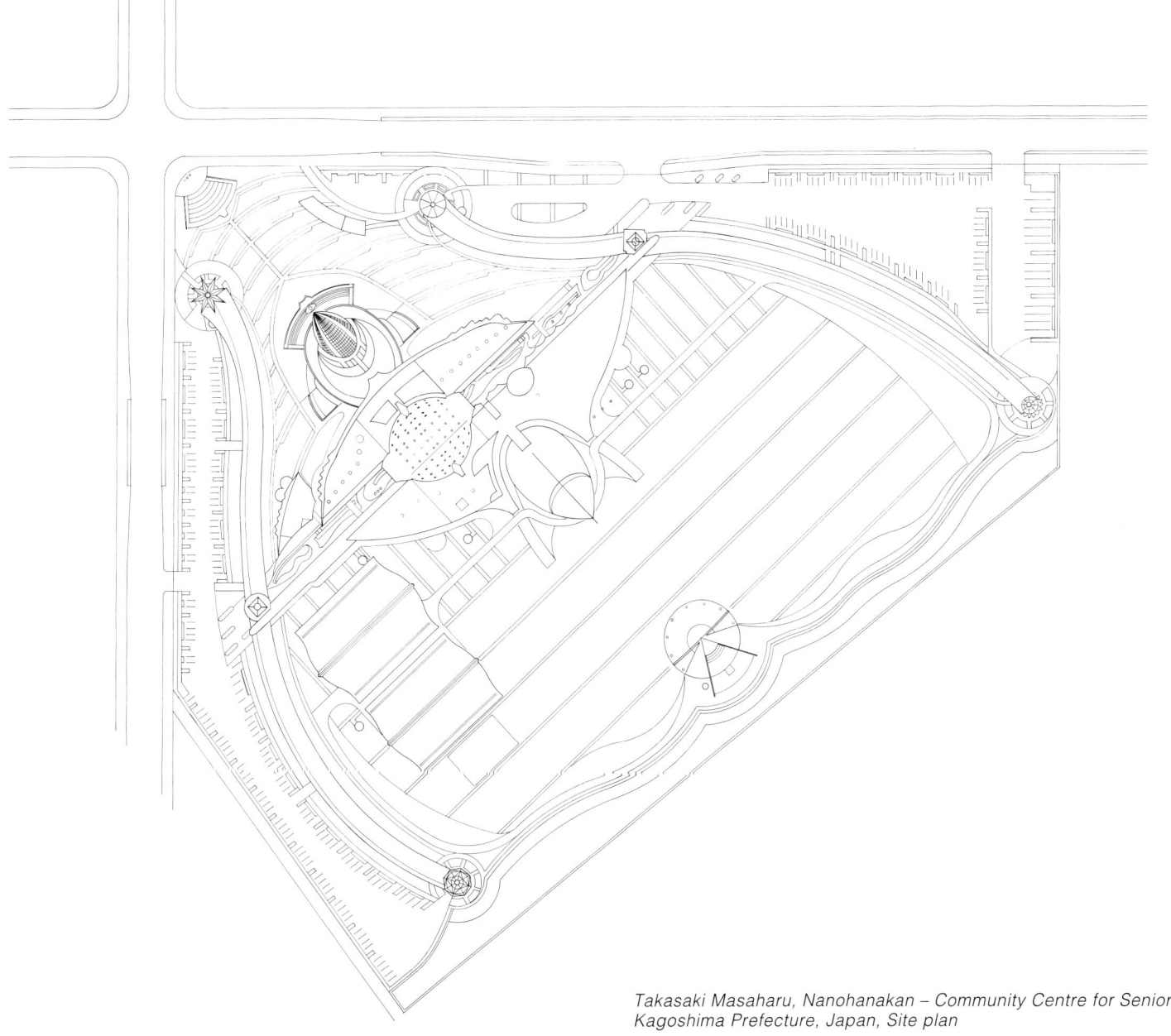

Takasaki Masaharu, Nanohanakan – Community Centre for Seniors, Kagoshima Prefecture, Japan, Site plan

RACHEL ARMSTRONG
SCIENCE-FICTION ARCHITECTURE

Using the real world as its starting point, the science-fiction genre creates alternative, radically different and hypothetical worlds, inspired by the conventions of science. As applied to architecture, science fiction is an imaginative form of design that interprets a fictional vision into a strategy for approaching a new problem, or inventing for future communities.

The inspiration that science has offered to creative practices this century is its promise to give modern society the power to control its environment and in doing so, to shape its destiny. Classical scientific theory suggests that the cosmos is reducible into its elements and that these can be reconstituted in their original form once their nature and behaviour are fully understood. Using a scientific method based on observation, analysis, reason, and experimentation, creative practices are able to extrapolate on new trends in scientific research and incorporate their own predictions on the evolution of the human body and technological invention.

Underpinning classical scientific philosophy is the Cartesian system of rational thought, first proposed by the mathematician, physiologist and philosopher René Descartes (1596-1650). He believed that the processes of human life, with the exception of mental functions, could be explained by the simple application of physical laws, and through an understanding of the structure of matter. He outlined a mechanistic model, which was subsequently applied to all scientifically observable phenomena, that required the *homunculus* ('little man') to operate the mechanisms of life using the new tools and techniques of science. The principles of science promised control over the building blocks of life and enabled designers, artists, and architects to work with scientific researchers to build a new society where, together, they would be able to address those problems that had afflicted people since the beginning of time. Man-made design and 'unnatural' interventions would secure a better quality of life and might even conquer death. In short, humans could play God.

In the light of new human knowledge, scientifically manufactured 'Edens' were created by human designers, and imaginary new worlds were inspired by the hitherto unknown territories discovered in explorations of the New World. Sir Thomas More's tract, *Utopia* (1516), for example, portrayed a civilisation that conducted itself according to the noblest 'scientific' qualities of humankind: pure logic and reason. Its architects were the first ecological conservators:

... among the Utopians all things are so regulated that men very seldom build upon a new piece of ground; and are not only very quick in repairing their houses, but show their foresight in preventing their decay: so that their buildings are preserved very long, with but little labor, and thus the builders to whom that care belongs are often without employment, except the hewing of timber and the squaring of stones, that the materials may be in readiness for raising a building very suddenly when there is any occasion for it.

The first novel to locate a Utopian city in the future was Louis Sebastien Mercier's *Memoirs of the Year Two Thousand Five Hundred* (1771). Taking Paris as his model, he improved the city through anticipated developments in human reason, science, and technology.

In the 20th century, mechanised individuals, under the control of god-like, human scientists were the natural inhabitants of these rationalistic worlds. The term 'robot' was invented by the Czech dramatist Karel Capeck in his play *RUR*, initials that stood for Rosum's Universal Robots. This personal vision of machines that were able to do everything a human could but without error, set the tone for the inhabitants of a scientifically advanced society and underlined the economic dynamics inherent in it.

RUR suggested that the scientific progress driving the industrial revolution was turning human workers into mere components of industrial machinery, destined either to die out or be physically absorbed into the factories. An increasing number of authors showed a similar scepticism in relation to scientific progress, prophesying dystopian provinces based on the real world. Their futuristic visions were provocative social commentaries on the striking inequalities evident in the newly industrialised urban environments.

One such cautionary tale was the silent film *Metropolis*, directed by Fritz Lang in 1926. Set in 2026, it portrays a cold mechanical, industrial city of the future brought to life by the architecturally trained Lang with suspended streets, zigzag buildings and a magnificent orange Olympic stadium. The narrative relies on imagery alone, painting a complex picture of a world in which the populace is separated into surface and subterranean dwellers. The privileged elite enjoy a luxurious existence, surrounded by beautiful gardens and arenas, and served by voluptuous yet soulless female robots. The lower class, meanwhile, live and work underground, enslaved by the machines that provide the power to run the infrastructure above. Curiously, this model is reflected in the direct relationship between prestige and elevation in modern skyscrapers.

Metropolis betrays an anxiety about the uncontrolled expansion of the human population on earth. As early as 1863, with his series of *Voyages Extraordinaires*, the visionary Jules Verne had already fantasised that travellers could embark on adventures to the centre of the earth, the bottom of the sea, or to the moon. The first use of special effects to depict a lunar landing was made by the avant-garde filmmaker Georges Méliès in *Trip to the Moon*, 1902. His use of expressionist techniques away from narrative and realist modes of representation was to influence sci-fi designers in the building of experimental worlds out of unconventional materials.

In the latter part of the 20th century, classical science has evolved into a pluralistic modern science drawing new inspiration from scientific discovery and a diversity of non-scientific disciplines. The greatest changes have taken place in physics and mathematics, accelerated by space travel, the advent of computers and the discovery of a new universe in virtual reality or cyberspace.

The construction of the built environment in uncharted territories came under serious consideration with the advent of missiles, rockets and space exploration in the 1960s. Following the first lunar landing in 1969, other major extra-terrestrial milestones included the successful orbit of the space station, Skylab, in 1973 and the first reusable space transportation system, the Space Shuttle. These events were anticipated by an explosion of fic-tional space adventures, most notably Stanley Kubrick's epic *2001: A Space Odyssey*. This painterly film not only influenced many subsequent movies including the *Star Wars* trilogy, but also inspired contemporary architects and designers. Kubrick's odyssey symbolises the next leap forward in man's evolutionary destiny, heralded by strange, alien obelisks. The prospect of life in space represented an ideal that gave humankind the chance to start yet again without the baggage inherited from the existing physical limitations of earth's environments.

The figure of the alien has been a dominant cultural element since the 1950s. Arthur C Clarke's *Rama* and Ian M Banks' *The Culture* trilogy portray alien civilisations as a complex relationship between societies and their architecture. Whilst Rama's inhabitants are reminiscent of primeval life, *The Culture* describes an advanced society located on an artificial planet. The inhabitants adopt thinly disguised socialist principles, enjoying leisure, and intellectual challenge as motivation.

The successful television series 'The X-Files' highlights the emerging 'New Age' science versus classic rationalism in the relationship between its main characters, Fox Mulder and Dana Sculley. The central premise is that the FBI has accumulated a group of dossiers relating to bizarre incidents, whose data reveals a set of basic patterns relating to alien abduction. Although the events have been known for decades, there has been a cover-up by the political and military establishments. The

precise motives and extent of this are unclear, but the conspiracy is wide enough to constitute a 'secret government' of the USA. The FBI facilitates the obsessive quest of Agent Mulder to prove the existence of aliens. The sceptical Sculley assists him, keeping a cooler, more rational approach to each crisis by applying methodological analysis to every improbable event. Sculley is more than another female sidekick: she represents the classical scientific approach that contrasts with Mulder's new-age acceptance of the possibility of emotional, improbable and imaginary events. The slogans 'Trust No One' and 'The Truth Is Out There' are ironic statements on the nature of observed phenomena, implying that there is no system of investigation that can determine The Real Truth.

These later sci-fi works convey a highly integrated relationship between human, machine, artifice and nature in inner and outer space. In this new interaction between humans and their environment, a more fluid relationship is portrayed, in which the homunculus is not in control but is absorbed into the matrix of these systems.

The increasing automation of future cities is taken to extremes in a number of narratives in which cities continue to thrive after their inhabitants have returned to a more primitive existence. Such near-deserted cities are featured in *Strength of Stones* (1981), by Greg Bear, and in Elizabeth Vonarburg's *The Silent City* of the same year, whilst cities that have undergone radical transformations using nano-technology are described in Kathleen Ann Goonan's *Queen City Jazz* (1994). These prophetic environments suggest that a new form of science fiction is emerging that will continue to inspire architects. New edifices will operate according to fresh, interconnected scientific theories and 'soft science' disciplines, prompted to move beyond the conventional designs of Modernist, mechanical structural shells that are under the direct control of homuncular human operators. An evolutionary transition in architectural design will replace classically scientific fossils with intelligent, responsive, fluid interfaces that both inform and learn from their organic inhabitants.

KARIN DAMRAU

BEYOND SOLIDITY

Inventions, Spaces and Concepts for the Elements of Air and Water

If one wished to break away from the traditional, Modernist architectural education in favour of experimentation, if one wished to look out over its limitations and constraints, and if one wished to seek an area as unfamiliar as possible, how would one start on this journey into the unknown?

A possible answer lies in the exploration of elements other than earth. During an experimental year in London, I have investigated different ways of designing architecture for, or with the qualities of, an alien medium. The first two designs were situated within the media themselves. The 'Tool for the City Dweller to Enter the Untamed Space' is a device to unite Man with the sea. A special hull transmits unknown perceptions from the world, under water to the traveller. The 'Los Angeles City Toy' – a swarm of flying objects situated above the city – changes its position and constellation according to the products (light, sound, temperature) of its inhabitants. Because of its presence, stories are created, which are passed on from area to area within the city. The project for a spa for London, situated on the earth/water surface of the River Thames, ended up on a much more abstract and atmospheric level. It hints at aspects of endlessness, nuances of different densities and a free movement in the three-dimensional space, where one could get lost in time. Simultaneously, it deals with site and practical use. As a result, it reaches a further limit – the limit between pure experiment and function.

These works that lie in the elements of air and water imply the dream of flying, or of being a fish; of being able to free oneself from earthboundness, to break away from foundation and gravity. Thus, they are suspended in a three-dimensional space. They are concerned with a flight away from the familiar, restrictive element of earth towards an alien medium without bounds. This essay deals with Mankind's dream of entering into a diverse medium, concentrating on the characteristics of the elements, on their portrayal in architecture, and on attempts to conquer these characteristics through technology, such as the conquest of the air by the aeroplane in order to achieve the freedom of the birds. We know that this dream has been in existence since at least the beginning of recorded history.

As Clive Hart relates in his book, *The Dream of Flight*,[1] many ancient civilisations endowed their heroes and gods in myths, legends and religion with the ability to fly through the air – notably the classical figures of Daedalus and Icarus. Evidence of this is also provided by examples from China and the Orient to Mexico, Egypt and Babylon. The winged figures of angels in Christianity are well known, and God is always depicted in His throne above the earthly realms. In most ancient philosophies, the air and the sky are given divine attributes. Despite a historic fear of the wrath of the gods, mankind sees the heavens as positive elements evoking paradise, redemption, freedom, spirituality.

The situation with water is more ambivalent. History gives us fewer examples of attempts to plumb the depths than of those to conquer the skies. This could be explained by something other than the fact that water has always been more accessible to mankind. In myth and legend, monsters and gods lived side by side in the sea, uniting the menacing and the divine. According to many stories of the Creation, before the world came into being there was only water. Greek mythology, for example, tells of the immense River Oceanus, which formed a liquid belt around the universe with neither a source nor an outlet, and gave birth to all the rivers and the entire sea. According to Genesis the world was born when 'darkness was upon the face of the deep. And the spirit of God moved upon the face of the waters'.

But, as Ulrike Brunotte points out, this 'fertile and life giving substance is... conceived as having originally been formless and chaotic, and is thus endowed with frightening and destructive properties'.[2] In Christianity, 'water symbolism, constantly fluctuating between the Great Flood and baptism' has been maintained up to the modern era. The chaotic state of water is also often compared with human madness, since water is traditionally seen as the mirror of the soul.

How did these ideas of air and water express themselves visually? What have artists, inventors, theologians, architects, Utopians and storytellers designed for these floating sanctuaries? Do these means of expression differ from those for the land? Have they succeeded in realising the dreams of mankind, or have the fruits of these desires set themselves apart from the fantasy?

Air and water

The comparison between the elements of air and water has been made again and again, particularly since nature has been studied in greater detail. Archimedes made an important point in his 'principle concerning the floating of bodies in liquids or gases', conceived approximately 250 years BC when he stated that floating materials – a ship in the sea for example – contained an upward pressure of liquid or gas, even when completely covered by fluid. In later centuries this law was applied to the air by several scientists and philosophers. John Wilkins, the Bishop of Chester, for instance, published in 1648 his *Mathematica Magick*, in which he put forward the thesis that the air 'has an upper surface, like the sea', and that 'the flotation principle of Archimedes could somehow be applied to the air'. Thus 'a vessel filled with... ethereal air would float on it as a boat on water'. Possibly for this reason many early plans for aircraft, such as Francesco de Lama's 1670 design for an 'aerial ship', as he himself called it, took the basic form of those used for water craft. Even today the word 'airship' is still used. Although there was never any attempt to construct it, this machine was a milestone in aeronautical history because it was one of the first steps towards the balloon. Besides this, it had all the characteristics of a ship, propelled forward by a sail. The design was based on models from nature with the power of flight, and built upon early knowledge of physics.

Many attempts to design a flying machine were doomed to failure from the start because observations made on the behaviour of physical bodies or living things in the water were applied to the air. Leonardo da Vinci made extensive observations on bird flight before drawing up his treatise 'Volo degli Ucelli' in 1505. He came to the conclusion, on the basis of the similarities between flying and swimming, that birds flap their wings in a downward and backwards direction, which would force the air, like the water, against the direction of movement. In the design for his ornithopter Leonardo therefore included wings that flap in a backward direction. In fact, birds flap their wings downward and forwards. The only design in which he digressed from imitating living creatures was one for a helix-driven helicopter of which it is said a model did successfully fly.

The filmmaker, Peter Greenaway, who has a passion for the theme of air and water, swimming and flying, falling and drowning, found a close poetic connection between the elements. His exhibition 'Flying over Water', held in 1997 was devoted to this theme.[3] He described Icarus as the first mythological hero who united the elements by falling from the sky to the sea. The attempt to defy gravity, to develop and behave independently in a universal, infinite, three-dimensional space is the basic common ground between the elements.

The professional journal *Quaderns* recently came up with a striking comparison between water and earth. All the characteristics attributed here to the water can also be applied to the air:

WATER	LAND
Universal medium	local medium
movement	roots
flow	solidity
infinite	memory
abstract shape	proximity
no points of reference	a codified, figurative landscape[4]

Perhaps the characteristics attributed to water are the qualities that seem 'easy' to us, bringing 'liberation'. If this is so, this comparison could inspire us to invent something that would distinguish a piece of architecture in the air from one on the ground. It would be universal, rootless, and would relate to the forces from which it is formed. It would refer to the boundlessness of its medium and it would perhaps be a place for nomads, a place that embodies the 'drifter'.

Myths, legends, religion – the first dreams of diving and flight

Man has always been profoundly impressed by the ease with which birds move through the air. Heroes and gods were therefore endowed with the wings of birds, in most cases attached in a symbolic way rather than aerodynamically. Hermes, the messenger of the gods, needed only winged sandals and petasus to enable him to glide easily through the air. In literature,

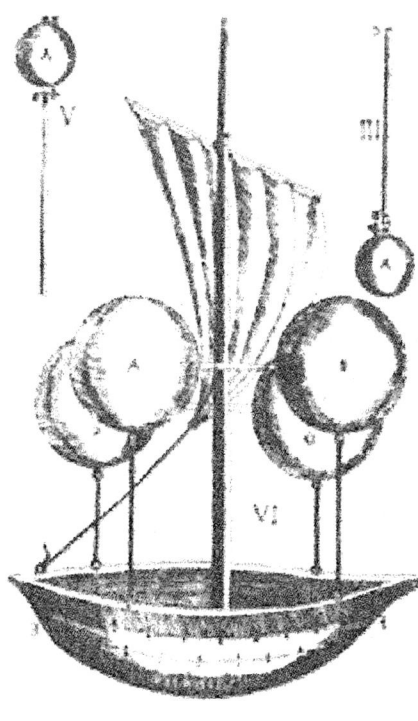

ABOVE: Daedalus and Icarus by Marie Briot,1638; BELOW: Francesco de Lana's design for an aerial ship,1670

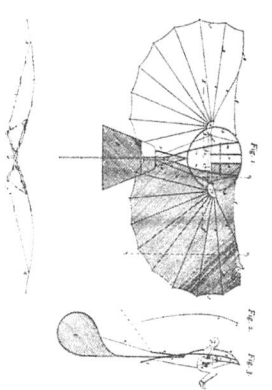

other examples show figures without wings, transported through the air by flying beasts or birds. They are often seated in a basket or chariot, tethered to flying creatures. The history of Alexander from the Middle Ages describes the trick he used to induce his griffins to fly: he held pieces of meat aloft on his sword, and when they smelled the meat they rose up in order to eat. One of the rare cases in early religion and myth in which a self-propelled vehicle appears is the legend of the Emperor Ki-Kung-Shi, whose chariot is depicted in a wood engraving by Tú Shu Tsi Chéng. Its two wheels resemble a waterwheel, set in motion by the 'rolling clouds', as if in a moving landscape. Who has not dreamt of being able to scale this changing mountain of clouds?

Just as heroes and gods moved easily through the air with the aid of wings, the divinities and legendary figures of water and the seas were also equipped with the attributes of their element. In Greek mythology Poseidon, the Lord of the Sea, and Triton, his son, are half-man, half-fish: they can propel themselves through the water and live in the depths of the sea in a magnificent palace with walls of mother-of-pearl and gardens of coral.

If myths and legends attest to, and embody, human hopes and fears, these few examples describe basic human dreams, such as living suspended under water or being carried along in the boundless realm of the air. However, until the beginning of the modern era, attempts to realise these dreams were considered reprehensible on religious grounds, particularly by Christians who felt that efforts to get closer to godly attributes were blasphemous.

Wish-machines from the Renaissance to Lilienthal

Between the Renaissance and the first successfully realised and controlled glider flight by Otto Lilienthal in 1895, mankind devoted an enormous amount of imaginative skill to the invention of flying and diving machines. The Renaissance – the beginning of knowledge, rationality and the transition from myth to human reason – was the time when Man began to use his intelligence to invent his world without fear of divine intervention. This enabled him to enter places that had previously been deemed the domain only of God. Man started to become the creator of his own world and observation of nature had an important role to play.

For Leonardo, as we have seen, bird flight was the key to the air. Nature was the ideal blueprint, which should be imitated in detail. Although a number of diving bells had already appeared in a legend of Alexander the Great in 332 BC, it was Leonardo again who made an exceptional innovation in this field. Around 1500 he was asked by the Venetians to design an underwater breathing device to be used in the war against Turkey. What he conceived was more advanced than anything known at that time: a self-contained underwater breathing apparatus, it was a forerunner of modern diving equipment. This invention was never built or tested. Today we know that it could not have worked because of the water pressure, which would have collapsed the

animal-skin air bag, and because it is not possible repeatedly to breathe the same air. Despite his erroneous observations and the fact that his flying machines 'are both wrong in principle and hopelessly impractical' as Hart explains, his designs seemed to represent a turning point in the quest for mastery of the elements. Though 'scientific' experiments, they embodied so much from mythology, so much from the pure dream of being able to move as freely as a bird, that they greatly attracted later artists, inventors and writers.

Vladimir Tatlin's design for a flying machine, *Letatlin* (1932), for example, bore a strong resemblance to da Vinci's ornithopter. It may be assumed that at a time when the secret of flight had already been revealed, if Tatlin was concerned to construct a working flying machine of this type, he wanted to convey a message about the old dream of mankind. In an interview with Zelinski in 1932 he gave an account of the work: 'I don't want this object to be approached in a purely utilitarian way. I created it as an artist... I consider it aesthetically perfect'.[5] But he went to great lengths to make *Letatlin* fly: 'I consider that my apparatus can also support a man in the air. I calculated the mathematical side, the resistance of the material, the surface of the wings'. Several Soviet pilots gave accounts of failed test flights, which finally left it severely damaged. In an essay on *Letatlin*, AA Strigalev comments: '...it is remarkable that he used not only the experiences of his contemporary, Lilienthal, but also those of Leonardo and even of the anonymous peasant who... jumped off a tall bell-tower in order to try out his home-made wings.[6] *Letatlin* can therefore be seen as the fantastic design of a man who primarily wanted to turn the dream of independent flight into reality. To this end, he not only followed the example of the latest scientific know-how, but also the dream-machines of great inventors from the history of flight.

Another student of Leonardo's designs is immortalised wearing his home-made wings in a painting on the library ceiling at the monastery of Schussenried in Württemberg. Named Kaspar Mohr, he was a Premonstratensian at the monastery of Schussenried, well known for his mechanical skills. Since studying Leonardo's flying machines around 1614, he had devoted himself to constructing one himself. It is revealing of the changing attitude of Christianity towards God´s medium in latter centuries to note the way in which he is portrayed on the monastery ceiling surrounded by angels with real wings.

Otto Lilienthal heralded real mastery of the air in 1895 with the first controlled flight in a glider. Century after century of attempts at flight had come to an end. One way of realising the dream had been found and from this moment the priority would be to improve upon it. Technology had dispelled the myths of air.

Demystification does, however, bring with it a loss – the loss of mystical ideas in favour of a scientific world, explicable by physics. 'Visions are sustained by desire... That which is envisioned can however lose its mystique when technological

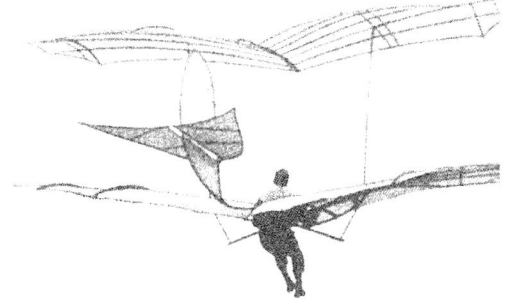

achievements undergo transition to social routine, from Icarus to Airbus, so to speak' wrote Herbert Lachmayer in 1996.[7] When the secret has been revealed, all that remains is to rationalise the process and adapt it to the latest scientific expertise. 'The second fall of Icarus took place at the moment when it had been forgotten which desire was motivating mankind when he dreamt of flying. Flying is not just flying.'[8] The first flying and diving machines embody the human feeling of elation resulting from finally achieving a genuine functioning result after centuries of experimentation. Meanwhile, however, the fact that Man can move around in alien elements with the aid of machines invented by himself is something that is taken for granted.

According to Robert McCarter, 'Technology and the machine were originally experimental in nature, but technology has since lost its experimental nature. A calculating, optimising, economising intention has taken over, and this narrow, utilitarian reasoning now determines the direction of what are still called research and invention'.[9] The main area to be refined was that of speed, ie advancement in aero- and hydrodynamics. Speed meant power, both economic and military, embodied in the rapid locomotion through a 'boundless' medium. Mastery of the laws of the air and the deep would soon be used for military purposes. Human inventions took on ominous characteristics. The ability to reach higher into the air abstracts the surface of the earth and makes it easier for warriors to launch their deadly weapons. Recently, the form of some vehicles of war in air and water, besides being shaped by aero/hydrodynamic considerations, has also been dictated by a completely different component: invisibility on the enemy's radar screen. When moulded by the laws of radar, ships and aircraft are remarkably similar.

In our world, dictated by rationality and economics, there is no place for that which is not practical. Usefulness is the measure for all things. Invention and research, above all, are under pressure from practicality and effectiveness. A logical step towards this end is the British-designed spacecraft 'Skylon'. It operates in lower earth-orbit, where it has less air resistance, making it highly effective and rapid over long-distance flights: it could fly from London to Australia in under two hours. Could this form of travel possibly become the social norm in the next millennium?

Amongst all these vehicles that pursue primarily economic goals there are, nevertheless, examples of an improvised, experimental nature, which came into being for completely different reasons. Two of these bear the names of mythological heroes who conquered alien elements. 'Pegasus' is an escape vehicle designed in 1968 by Bernd Böttger, one of the few who managed to flee to the West from the former GDR. He did this with the aid of a home-made vehicle, built in his basement workshop. This mechanism, which was able to carry him about one metre below the surface of the water, consisted of a two-stroke engine and a cigar-shaped container for fuel made of

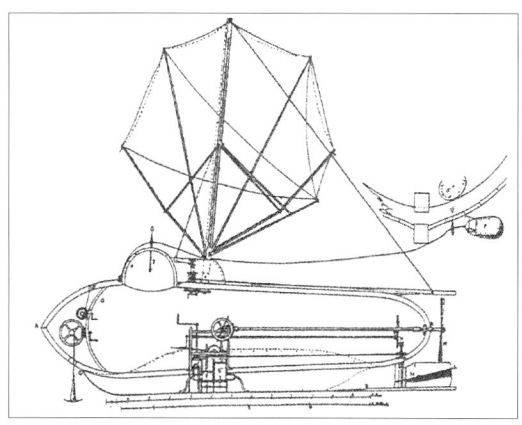

fibreglass. The engine drove a home-made propeller, and a snorkel secured the air supply to the carburettor. Professor F Müller of Berlin Technological University considered the invention to be 'as revolutionary as the moped or the diving suit, even better than both put together'.[10] It was certainly a machine that embodied the idea of a life of freedom.

Another experimental device is dedicated to Daedalus, who was also on the run, from the labyrinth of the Cretan King, Minos, resorting to home-made wings. The goal of the 'Daedalus 88' project, initiated by Massachusetts Institute of Technology (MIT) and carried out with the support of NASA, was to retrace Daedalus' route. Following decades of research, a micro-light construction was developed. It was driven by manpower, like a bike, the energy produced being transferred to the motion of a propeller. It weighed no more than 32 kilograms and had a wingspan of 34 metres. After careful observation of the weather, a route with an easy range was chosen. Following many test flights, 'Daedalus' started out from Crete, heading for Santorini. The vehicle remained in the air for three hours 54 minutes before it crash-landed in a gust of wind 10 metres off the coast of Santorini. The experiment was more or less successful and the design was a wonderful, up-to-date interpretation of the dream of self-powered, independent flight. Technology offered the opportunity to realise the dream whilst the main emphasis was on the interface between nature and technology, not on an attempt by technology to overcome nature. It is admirable that so much effort has gone into researching something that obviously has no 'practical' value in society. Despite the rationality of our world the old dreams are not forgotten.

The flying island and extraordinary journeys
Over the centuries, alongside real attempts to master elements beyond solidity, many literary works and fantasies have emerged that describe imaginary journeys through them. Some, including Jules Verne's *Voyages Extraordinaires*, took their inspiration from technological innovation. Portrayals of flying devices bore a strong resemblance to real designs for flying machines. Other writers abandoned themselves entirely to their fantasies. These novels seem to have jolted the inherent dream of humanity into life, in their turn inspiring new attempts at a solution by inventors. In 1790, for example, Father Laurenço de Gusmao, a Portuguese theologian and scientist, designed the 'Passarola' (great bird). It took the form of a boat with a bird's head and tail, and was centrally sustained by bird's wings. Attached at the front and the rear of the ship was an aerial sail, which spanned the pilot's cockpit. An engraving shows two additional terrestrial globes, which, according to the description of the author, encased large amber lodestones to lift the vehicle with the aid of magnetism. As CH Gibbs-Smith points out, this 'follows a popular trend of seventeenth-century fiction writers'.[11] In Jonathan Swift's *Gulliver's Travels* (1726), Gulliver journeys to the flying island of Laputa:

...a vast opaque body... a perfect circle, its diameter 7,837 yards... three hundred yards deep, on which lived a ruler who could punish the territory below by hovering over it and thus excluding the sunlight and rain, by flinging great stones down or even by descending and flattening the area.

Like the 'Passarola', of which Swift may well have had knowledge, the island could rise and descend with the aid of 'a loadstone of prodigious size'.

The novel *The Life and Adventures of Peter Wilkins*, by Robert Paltock, which appeared 24 years later, once again picked up on the idea and desire for independent flight. In the story, Peter Wilkins meets a female flying creature from the 'land of flight' – a Gawrey – and with her help reaches the country of the Glumms and Gawreys. The flying apparatus – called a 'graundee' – with which these creature are born and which enables them to fly, is a kite-like object fixed to their backs. It can also be used as a boat, and when not in use, can be shut or detached. Wilkins falls in love with the Gawrey and later marries her. His appearance in the 'land of flight' is to a certain degree a 'civilising mission', since the Glumms and Gawreys are 'noble savages' living in close relationship with the natural world.

More than a century later came the publication of Jules Verne's Voyages Extra*ordinaires*, running from 1863 until Verne's death in 1905 and spanning 62 volumes.

The unusual thing about Verne's *Journeys* is the fact that they not only described a long or difficult passage, but also broadened human horizons, provided insight into the unknown and led into the elements which, according to the natural order of things, were inhabited by other species: the fish in the water, the birds in the air.[12]

Here, the heroes no longer simply move around the earth in the 'horizontal' plane, but travel in the 'vertical' dimension: through the air to the moon, through the depths to the bottom of the sea and to the centre of the earth, and even through time. These imaginary journeys awaken the great dreams of mankind.

Verne's heroes carry out their adventures with the aid of technological inventions based on existing innovations from the second half of the 19th century. The depiction of the helicopter 'Albatross' in *The Clipper of the Clouds* (1886), is practically identical to Gabrielle de la Landelle's design for an aerial vessel of 1863. Verne gave these real-life ideas for vehicles inexhaustible power to travel into and through the vertical plane. In doing so, he realised the technological dreams of mankind, discovering our world and presenting images of its demystification through the technological means of the future.

Imaginary inventions and journeys in novels can therefore be seen to have a dynamic relationship with real inventiveness. The novel uses genuine technological blueprints for inspiration, giving them a fantastical life, attempting to achieve the true fulfilment of the dreams of mankind. This in turn stimulates the

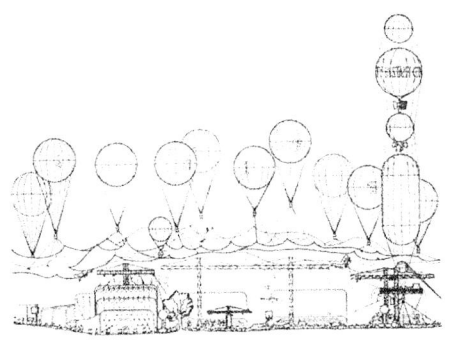

OPPOSITE LEFT: Satirical representation of a Utopian airship, late 18th century; OPPOSITE RIGHT: Laurenço de Gusmao's 'Passarola', 1709, from an engraving of 1714; LEFT: 'Instant City', Peter Cook, 1969

ambition of the inventor, who cannot fail to be inspired with ideas for realising these dreams. Invention is driven by a game of ping-pong between fantasy and transformation, between vision and technological tinkering. In an ideal situation, the architect can embody both poles.

Die Gläserne Kette and the Russian Utopists

Another writer whose tales and science-fiction stories took inspiration from the first successful experiments in flight was the Berliner, Paul Scheerbart. He portrayed visions of a society that knew how to put this achievement to a wonderful and enjoyable use. In *The Emperor of Utopia* (1904) for example, he described an air coach that was lifted into the air by flexible wings and propellers at the back, and to make the departure more comfortable, 'tube-like-legs' were extended mechanically during the first stages of departure. In a chapter entitled 'The Artist's Celebration', a grandiose party takes place in over 20 air-restaurants, which are lifted by large balloons, outlandishly illuminated at night.[13] The party and its arrangement in the air are an embodiment of the ideas of the 'counter movement', which opposed the fashion to favour the 'ancient'. The counter movement's notion of the future 'was to be distinguished in particular by transportable houses – and, indeed, by transportable cities', as Scheerbart described it. These stories made 'the charm of transportable architecture evident', and in the words of Ulrich Conrads, inspired 'a whole generation of artists, especially architects, to airy, colourful and weightless looking exercises on movement and balance'.[14] The fascinating new aspects here were grace, agility and, above all, boundlessness:

> We want no walls that completely exclude the outside world – like the old masonry walls; we want brilliantly colourful, transparent, double glass walls... We want walls that do not shut us from the great, infinite universe. Boundlessness is greatness supreme – let us never forget it. And boundlessness is the endless space of the cosmos. Nevermore shall we allow ourselves to be separated from it. This is why we want glass architecture to vanquish all the rest.[15]

Scheerbart's works were serialised in *Frühlicht*, the architecture magazine of his close friend, Bruno Taut, who founded Die Gläserne Kette (The Glass Chain), a Utopian group of architects, artists and writers. In 'Die Auflösung der Städte' (The Disintegration of Cities), he channelled the spirit of Scheerbart's ideas of weightlessness, boundlessness and the formation of unity with the cosmos into visionary architectural drawings. 'Das Karussell' (The Carousel), of 1920, for example, is a cosmic, comic aerial object in silver captioned: 'On a large sphere are rows of seats, one above the other. It is being carried by aeroplanes and is rotated by propellers in the wind – planes disguised as comets zoom around the carousel'. 'The Disintegration of Cities' is, 'of course, only a Utopia and a little amusement', claimed Taut, 'a way to "Alpine Architecture"'.[16]

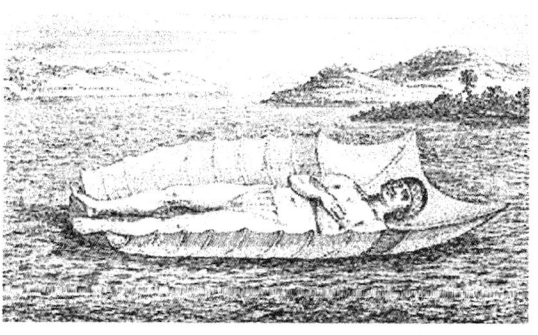

ABOVE: 'The Little Town of Laputa', engraving in Gulliver's Travels, *Johnathan Swift, 1726*; BELOW: Floating Glumm in Robert Paltock's The Life and Adventure of Peter Wilkins, *1750*

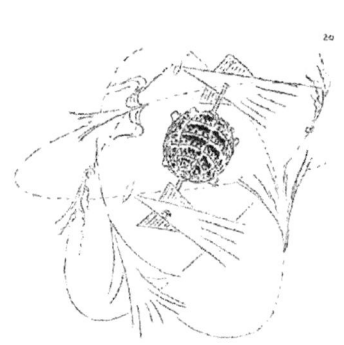

Wenzel Hablik was another participant of Die Gläserne Kette who translated his dreams of 'castles towering above clouds' and the ideas of the 'imaginary architects' into drawings. He formulated his interest in natural phenomena as a 'creative force' and the desire to bond with the cosmos. The drawing entitled 'The Building of an Air Colony', depicting six balloon-like forms, bound together in the shape of a circle, was produced as early as 1908. His 'Technical Island' and 'Discoverer's Colony' bring to mind crystalline architecture.

Die Gläserne Kette had no ambition actually to realise their plans for the air. The designs were an idealised expression of a world outlook and a quality of boundlessness, independence and weightlessness, unity with the cosmos and nature as a formative power – all the characteristics available to living things in the media of air and water of which humanity has dreamt for so long. According to Scheerbart, the attempt was to transfer these characteristics onto the earth, to transform them into glass architecture that was no longer separate from the cosmos.

Almost simultaneously, in Russia, there was a different reaction to successful human flight: a strong, inspirational belief that many visions would soon be transformed by technology.

> Towns in the air; towns of glass and asbestos; towns on springs; what are they – eccentricity, tricks, desire to be original? No, they are simply optimised purposefulness.
> In the air – in order to free the earth.
> Made of glass – to be filled with light.
> Asbestos – to reduce the structures weight.
> On springs – to achieve balance.[17]

In this way Boris I Arvatov defended the radical designs for future cities in the Soviet Union. Stimulated by the Revolution of 1917, many contemporary architects and social theoreticians thought that the future was not Utopian, but 'within the reach of the present'.[18] The new scientific and technological achievements of the previous years sent a whole generation into euphoria, giving them faith in the potential of technology to bring further revolutionary discoveries and inventions. During the 1920s this awareness of the implication of scientific discoveries for a different future gave rise to Soviet science fiction. Novels and short stories explored scientific possibilities as well as socio-political changes. Following these examples, architects of the Soviet Union created imaginative and far-reaching experimental projects. These symbolised on the one hand a new political structure – Socialism and Communism – and on the other, as a promised result of this, new achievements in technology that would provide the realisation of these visions. It was believed that there would be a the new social order throughout the world and that, as a kind of 'prerequisite' to it, the latest technological achievements would be available to everyone.

'Technology creates wonders. Architecture also must create wonders', Nikolai Ladovski wrote on a note attached to his drawings shown at the Nineteenth State Exhibition in Moscow.[19]

His experimental projects should be viewed against this background. Some of them refer to the topic of Soviet science fiction, as was reflected by the student projects, 'Flying City', of his pupil Georgy Kruitkov in 1928. In these, he proposed not only to lift buildings above the earth's surface, but also to free them from any fixed location. The earth was to be cleared of habitation, and reserved for work, nature and recreation. The dwellings of the Flying City were arranged in a strict order: in 'tiers along a notional surface of a paraboloid'.[20] To ensure communication between the floating dwellings and the ground he devised a universal form of transport to be used by a single person: the 'cabin', which was capable of travelling through the air, on the ground, on and under water. The mobile cabins could easily be linked into each dwelling by niches reserved for this purpose. To realise his project, Kruitkov assumed that in the future atomic energy would easily provide the power to lift the cities into the air. A year later Viktor Kalmykov – another pupil of Ladovsky – suggested in his student work, 'Sarturnii', the construction of a circular city around the equator. Raised above the ground, it orbits the globe at the speed of the earth's rotation.

Both designs could be seen in one way as a reinterpretation of Ebenezer Howard's garden-city concept, which was a major part of early Soviet experiments in town-planning, due to its concept of a 'socialist-settlement'. The earth's surface remained untouched in both projects and was owned by everybody for the enjoyment of nature. In another way, they embodied the idea of a new world order for society: the cities could spread out over the whole world in order to free it for Socialism and Communism. Cities – and their political ideals – would no longer be fixed to a particular site, they would be situated in an ideal physical environment, a universal environment. In Kruitkov's work, however, the structure of the city itself was in a strict order – the position of the single dwelling was under the control of the structure as a whole. In a way this posed a contradiction: the potential for universality was undermined by the arrangement of the city for a specific physical position in a strange parabolic form. The buildings, by contrast, were organised as if on the ground: arranged in storeys with balconies – and in the case of Kalmykov, into a horizontal skyscraper.

In the case of the Russian utopists therefore, the medium of air was used more to demonstrate technological achievement (and power) and the idea of political world revolution, than to realise the dream of independent flight or to provide man with aerial qualities. The projects in the air mirrored the social ideas of Communism, such as the equality of dwelling conditions, and freeing the earth from any one owner, so that it could be used by all. It is fascinating that all these projects were so courageous in drawing and translating contemporary visions into architecture. They should be seen as milestones in architectural thinking. It is only a pity that these ideas could not really continue in the aftermath of the disillusionment with technological advance, in

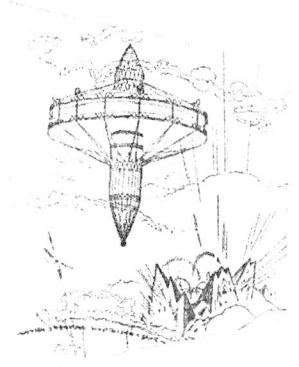

OPPOSITE LEFT: 'Das Karussel', in 'Die Auflösung der Städte', Bruno Taut, 1920; OPPOSITE RIGHT: 'Technical Island', Wenzel Hablik; LEFT: 'Discoverer's Colony', Wenzel Hablik

contrast to those of Die Gläserne Kette, which were not dependent upon the prospect of scientific changes.

The Architecture of Transition

With the first experiences of flight there was a change not only in the opportunity for experiencing the air, but also for viewing the earth. Soon, the consequences for architecture were discovered and described. In an article entitled 'Luftschiffahrt und Architekten', Fritz Wichert stated: 'The shackles of gravity are loosening... For our architectural outlook this literally means a revolution... The roof of a house takes on a totally different significance... it takes on formal value. Roofs become fronts.[21] When man achieved the ability to fly, space was perceived in a new way. 'Gravity-architecture', as Christoph Asendorf referred to it in his *DAIDOLOS* article, 'Fluctuation of Forms' (15 September, 1990), was overcome, or was considered in relative terms. Artists and architects are still formulating new models for spatial design in relation to the discovery of the fifth elevation.

An artist whose work embodied these new experiments was the Russian, Alexander Rodchenko. His concept of 'top elevation' from 1920, was emphasised in a project to design a future city in which the buildings would be composed as upended pyramids. On the one hand this would save ground, and on the other, the fifth elevation would be the most important. Therefore, his series of sketches for buildings with 'top elevations' had an expressive roof design that could be viewed from the air.

Kasimir Malevich also demanded that the fifth elevation should be taken into account. He, however, went a step further with Suprematism, wishing to free his architecture from vertical earthly gravity. In 'Fluctuation of Forms', Asendorf quotes Malevich:

The attainment of weightlessness is the 'highest aim of technology. In the spiritual realm man is weightless'. Both human spheres of the mind and outer space are governed by the same laws, they know neither ceiling nor floor, only multi-directional motion – 'what, then do space, size and weight mean?' Malevich links mystic experience to the utopia of a technology which in a revolutionary way overcomes earthly realities.

This describes perfectly what the interpretation of the new flying experiment could mean for architecture. The desire was to gain a condition in which Man could behave as he does in his mind: without gravity, without set ideas about up and down (ceiling and floor) and without a fixed position in space. However, one could call into question why Malevich in his 'Planet House' for a pilot interpreted this aim as an aeroplane-like but rather conventional building. Though it had no foundations, the layout was still 'normal'. Perhaps this teaches us that the desire for weightlessness might be better achieved by freeing architecture from the well-defined organisation of ceiling and floor and from the conventional line between outside and inside than by a technical endeavour to achieve weightlessness in the real sense.

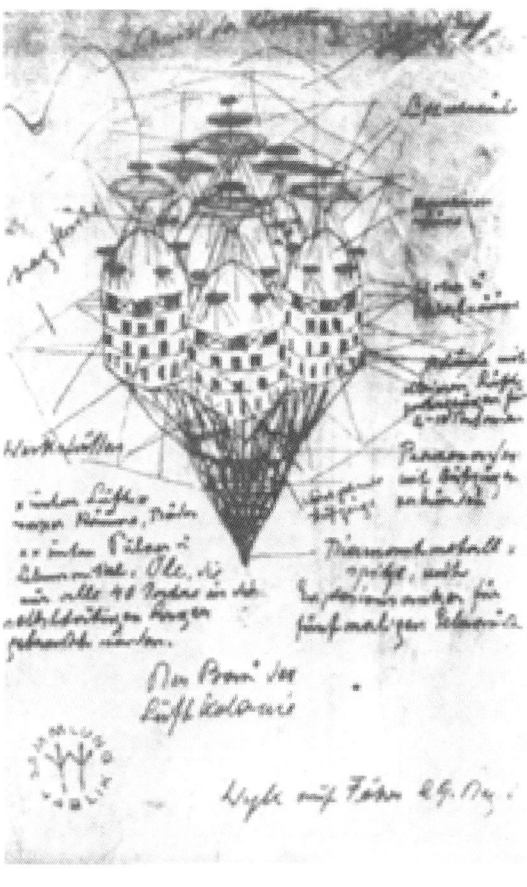

'The Building of the Air Colony', Wenzel Hablik, 1908

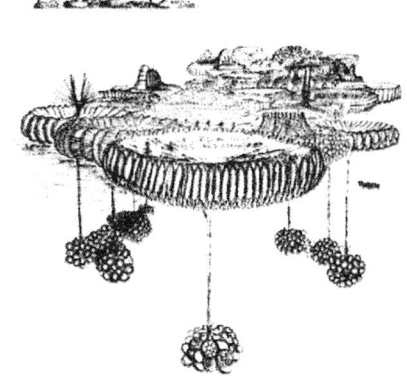

Rainer Stommer has described El Lissitzky's *Sky-hook* as 'the architecture of transition'.[22] This description presents one of the two possible solutions for the desire to interpret the qualities of flight and suspension architecturally. The architecture of transition is an architecture that is linked to the earth by its supports, but hints at the possibility of rising completely above it; it is in a state of 'transition' – no longer really earthbound but not yet totally suspended. Lissitzky saw strong parallels between the evolution of Man's transport systems and architecture. As Rodchenko did, he assigned the architecture of the pyramid, with its strong foundations, to the past. To the present he assigned the skeleton-construction, as an expression of the opportunity to travel on the earth's surface. The man who has the ability to fly has to overcome foundations and must define a new kind of architecture for this condition. Do we draw the conclusion that flight is possible by the suspension of architecture, that architecture should literally fly? With his Sky-hook, Lissitzky, along with his Russian contemporaries, had faith in technology in order to realise a vision. But the dream of the endless technological revolution was soon shattered.

The transition of architecture and liquid ideas

If we turn round the expression 'the architecture of transition' into 'the transition of architecture', this could have the meaning of freeing architecture from the technical attempt to lift a construction into the air, in favour of gaining a taste of the qualities of air, and bringing these qualities down to earth and into architecture. One could argue that the building of an airport implies more qualities of 'weightlessness' than a strained and vain effort to raise something into the air.

To a certain extent, Le Corbusier's thoughts about the creations of modern industry could be included amongst examples of this transition of architecture. For example, he associated architecture with the forms of ships and aeroplanes, and demanded the abolition of foundations and the mastery of the earthbound. But in his mind, mastery of earthboundness didn't mean the abolition of gravity, but an opportunity to gain space. He raised the ground floor of his buildings so that the only connection with the ground was the supports. He thus produced new possibilities for designing the ground, but it was never his intention literally to lift his buildings into the air. In this way he used certain aspects of 'flight' or 'suspension', which constitute a transition of architecture; they bring qualities of air or water into architecture in a figurative sense.

Le Corbusier used these aspects of 'suspension' in a rational way. He was not talking about 'flight-qualities'. In his opinion, the aeroplane had to be regarded exclusively as a machine. In *Towards a New Architecture*, 1923, he described what the aeroplane could teach architects:

The lesson of the aeroplane is not primarily in forms it has created, and above all we must learn to see in an aeroplane

not a bird or a dragon-fly, but a machine for flying; the lesson of the aeroplane lies in the logic which governed the enunciation of the problem and which led to its successful realisation.

The unattainable desire to enter the air as a problem; the machine to fly as its solution; the need to dwell as a problem; the machine to live as its solution; the wish to travel faster as a problem; the automobile as a solution: the examples are interchangeable:

The aeroplane shows us that a problem well stated finds its solution. To wish to fly like a bird is to state the problem badly, and Ader's 'Bat' never left the ground. To invent a flying machine having in mind nothing alien to pure mechanics... was to put the problem properly: in less than ten years the whole world could fly.

The aeroplane, ship and automobile were used to describe what the new aesthetics of architecture should be: a rational solution of a problem with the 'honest' aesthetics of modern industry.

As we have seen, the transition of architecture can be defined as a form of design that brings 'aerial' or 'fluid' qualities into the human habitat. Some aspects of these qualities are universality, movement, flow, infinity, abstraction. Amongst the architects whose works attempt this are Haus-Rucker-Co and Coop Himmelb(l)au. With its project 'Cloud', Coop Himmelb(l)au formulated new ideas on living in an extended area of perception. Similarly, Haus-Rucker-Co's 'Air-Unit' can be attached to all types of building. They describe it as follows:

Air-Unit is a simulated housing unit. An air-conditioned capsule made of transparent foil forms a spherical living area... One is no longer tied to living in one plane, one can expand freely into space... floors out of nets, ropes, ladders and soft platforms become the basis for a new type of mobility.[23]

The thin exteriors could be considered as a refinement of Scheerbart's Glass Architecture ideas. The structure is like a climatic chamber, or one's own cosmos, separated from the great cosmos by only a membrane. The amorphous exterior moves in the wind, its spherical shape when inflated suggesting endlessness and unity with the universe.

In the course of the 20th century a 'fundamental crisis'[24] has occurred in the world of science. The image of the 'conventional science of lucidity' is being turned into the image of a 'science of complexity'[25] by theories such as Einstein's Theory of Relativity, the theory of complexity and chaos. A linear image of nature is being replaced by non-linearity. Nature is being recognised as independent and creative, 'a dynamic organism' rather than a 'dead machine'.[26]

According to Wolfgang Welsch in an account of Postmodernist thought in all disciplines that are demonstrating perspectives for the design of the future: 'Science itself tells us that... the physical nature of reality is not homogenous but heterogeneous, not

harmonious but dramatic, not uniform but diverse... '[27] The idea of heterogeneity, plurality and discontinuity runs through all disciplines subsequently illustrated by him, through the philosophies of Lyotard to Derrida, through literature and sociology. The desire to reproduce this outlook architecturally, to depict the dynamism of the world and all the processes going on within, takes models from nature and science and puts them into architecture. The goal here is to rid architecture of the static and the linear, which is in direct conflict with modern thought. Terms such as 'Liquid Architecture' emerge. The word 'liquid' is assigned to all possible situations: to information, forces and energies that are active and in motion in the urban environment. The concept of 'Liquid Architecture' is described in detail by Marcos Novak in his essay 'Liquid Architecture in Cyberspace':

> For the first time in history the architect is called upon to design not the object but the principles by which the object is generated and varied in time... A work of liquid architecture is no longer a single edifice but a continuum of edifices, smoothly or rhythmically evolving in both space and time. Judgements of a building's performance become akin to the valuation of dance and theatre.[28]

An architect who shares this view is the American, Greg Lynn. His architecture is generated with the aid of a computer programme called 'blob modeller'. This simulates a dynamic energy field in which various influences such as light, shade and the movement of people shape an object. The end product resembles a stone formed by water. Lynn describes the site itself as: 'a liquid medium with aqueous characteristics of flow and transformation in time'.[29] In this respect, he works indirectly with a 'liquid medium' that is only seen as such from a new perspective on the world, but at best his architecture hints at this without actually embodying it. It is not the characteristics of 'liquid' media that interest Lynn but interaction with them. His architectural works are photographs of an object formed by 'water', which changes with the direction of the current. It is questionable whether the object is formed by these locally active forces. Simply simulating the forces is just an architect's interpretation, which to a certain extent determines the result of the computer-generated image.

The recent work of Ben van Berkel is similar to Lynn's. He refers to forms of energy such as public, economic and political information as 'mobile forces'. But he goes one step beyond Lynn. His architecture also embodies the characteristics of the 'liquid' forces: 'The new architectural body, allowing for diversity, conflict, and change within itself, emanates qualities particular to our time, including vicariousness, transformability, and the almost limitless absorption of information'.[30] Berkel's 1995 entry for the competition to design Yokohama Port Terminal characterises the power of water. Computer graphics allow the observer to see directly into the interior of a room, which seems to blur into other rooms. The surfaces of this space are semi-transparent and it is difficult to say which levels belong to which area, which ones are

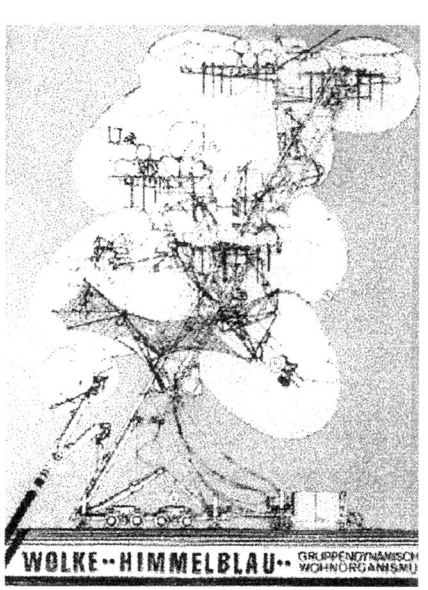

Coop Himme(l)blau, Cloud, 1968-72

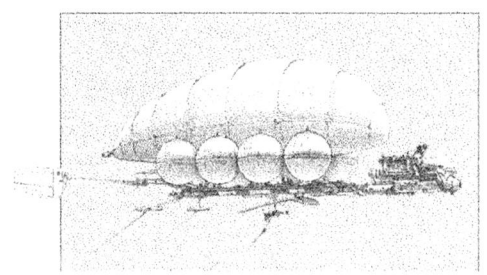

showing through from elsewhere, and whether or not they can be accessed. The surfaces are formed in such a way that it is not possible to make out their exact dimensions. It might even be the case that the whole surface is fluid. Walls and ceilings are made from one flowing mass; upper and lower surfaces are interchangeable. This does not overcome gravity but it does point to its dispersal. The question is whether the realisation of the object can sustain these qualities. In any case, this project comes close to the transition of architecture.

Lebbeus Woods' 'Turbulence-architecture' can be seen as a new way of describing reality as a field of effective fluid forces. Woods, however, does not work with a computer, but expresses the virtuality of energy flows in his drawings. 'Turbulence', he has said, is an architecture 'that arises from and sinks back into fluidity, into the turbulence of a continually changing matrix of conditions, into an eternal, ceaseless flux'.[31] In his drawings, the works of architecture emerge from a fluid field of structures. They are discernible by their greater surface area, but they have no beginning and no end. They are one with the 'changing matrix of conditions'. According to Woods they 'crystallise' out of the matrix just for a moment. Due to the fact that they are a part of the matrix, they also display all of its qualities. The structures do not portray any physical fluid medium, but in a figurative sense Woods' matrix possesses all such qualities, and more: the matrix embodies 'shifting forces... patterns of unpredictable movements... changes of mind, alterations of position, spontaneous disintegrations and syntheses... architecture drawing its sinews'. Besides this, 'Turbulence', like many of Woods' works, also has a socio-political dimension. 'Turbulence-architecture' is an 'architecture of gypsies' an 'architecture of migrants', and an 'architecture that insults politicians, because they could not claim it as their own'.

Woods' project, 'Aerial Paris', is also full of social elements. The objects floating in the sky over Paris are inhabited by autonomous individuals, who 'do not refer to past-future continuities or identities', and they – like the architecture itself – have won the fight over gravity. For gravity to Woods is 'an insidious enemy of the animate', which 'continuously drains the energies of living, animate things, as they struggle against it, in order to move and to live'.[32] The objects do not embody infinity; they have a beginning and an end. 'Made' out of metal and wood, they are heavy but have overcome gravity and float freely in space. They are not part of the medium in which they are situated, but they do carry something of the myth of the first flying machines, along with a sci-fi image. Unlike the flying objects in 'AEON 100', the objects in 'Aerial Paris' are not buoyed up by a supporting balloon but by huge pieces of fabric floating freely in the wind.

Science Fiction and the conquest of new media
Two newly discovered areas are currently offering Man the opportunity to move around in a weightless environment: outer space and cyberspace. In cyberspace, an artificial world has been created that is no longer subject to the laws of physics. Here we can at least create a visual impression of flying and floating through rooms as we please. Above all, though, we can also invent new environments: new physical environments, new material environments, new environments for time and new relationships with matter. According to Novak, architecture can be completely 'liquid' here:

In cyberspace a liquid architecture is clearly a dematerialised architecture. It is an architecture that is no longer satisfied with only space and form and light and all the aspects of the real world. It is an architecture of fluctuating relations between abstract elements. It is an architecture that tends towards music.[33]

'Cyberspace is the habitat for the imagination', he continues. This is reminiscent of Malevich's statement that the attainment of weightlessness is the 'highest aim of technology' and 'In the spiritual realm man is weightless'. This dream has not been realised in our habitat, as Malevich hoped, with the aid of technology, but technology has made it possible to create an artificial realm for the imagination.

In outer space we are weightless in the physical sense. Admittedly, the physical sensation of weightlessness is currently reserved only for the few, and the protective clothing into which we have to squeeze ourselves is still awkward and bulky, but everything will change. We can currently fly our space craft into space where our structures can expand in all directions, and we can extend this system of building blocks ad infinitum. Perhaps designs such as the one by Fritz Haller for a space station will be turned into reality and will expand our habitat out into space.

Man's experimentation with dreams of flight is still continuing in the fantastic world of science fiction. As Christian W Thomsen details in his book, *Visionary Architecture*, science fiction could at one time only be applied to literature, but this century broke through into 'film, music, painting, toys, record covers and computer games.'[34] If one skims through the *Star Wars* trilogy, for example, one sees that in these fantastic realms, flight is possible in every variation: in vehicles that move at the speed of light, in silently soaring boats resembling sailing ships, on the backs of strange creatures, in flying machines similar to those of Leonardo da Vinci, or in weightless, unsupported contraptions. Whole cities are primarily geared towards flight. The buildings often have enormous dimensions. They are intended to be perceived and used in the three-dimensional realm. The 'sand-sailing skiff' used on the planet Tatooine resembles the first airship designs from the 17th century. The 'Floating Health Spas' of the gas giant Bespin, where one can take a 'cloud bath', recapture the image of a gentle balloon ride, and many other flying devices are reminiscent of the architecture of Lebbeus Woods, who designed the architectural sets for David Fincher's film, *Alien III* (1992).

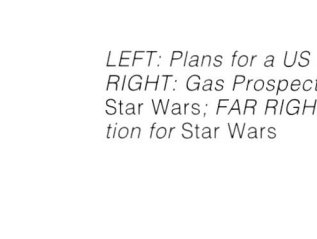

LEFT: Plans for a US space laboratory; RIGHT: Gas Prospector, illustration for Star Wars; *FAR RIGHT: Vehicle, illustration for* Star Wars

By dealing with new ways of creating architecture, we venture towards a limit. One possible position is to retain the architectural object, but allow it to be formed by fluid forces. By doing so, the effects created by the forces on the object are determined, or at least influenced, by the architect. The other strategy is to provide architecture with liquid characteristics. In the first case the architect retains his position as a creator and controls the result. In the second, the 'liquid reactions' achieve independence and the architect becomes an observer.

The question, therefore, is firstly, where exactly the limit lies between creating, designing and observing, and secondly, how one could transfer and translate 'fluid' qualities of these experiments into our experienced habitat. Besides researching the experimental limits, one could explore the limit between the tangible/experimental and the abstract/atmospheric further. Perhaps this area will provide new architectural possibilities that could enrich our habitat and our world.

Translated by Wendy Nowak

Notes

1 Clive Hart, *The Dream of Flight*, Faber & Faber (London), 1972.
2 Ulrike Brunotte in 'Water Catastrophes – Catastrophic Water. From the Flood to the Maelstrom', *DAIDALOS, Architecture Art Culture*, Bertelsmann-Verlag (Gütersloh),15 March, 1995, pp100-110.
3 Fundació Joan Miró, Barcelona.
4 *Quaderns d'Architectura i Urbanisme*, No 212, 'Tierra-Agua/Water-Land', Fonti Prat Associates (Barcelona), 1996, preface.
5 Corvina Kiadó, *Tatlin*, Thames & Hudson (London), 1988, p309.
6 Ibid p39.
7 Herbert Lachmayer, 'Vom Icarus zum Airbus' (From Icarus to Airbus), *Wunschmaschine – Welterfindung* (Dream Machines – World Invention), cat, Kunsthalle (Vienna), 1996, p24-39.
8 Thomas Macho, 'Träume sind älter als Erfindungen' (Dreams are older than inventions) *Wunschmaschine – Welterfindung*, p45-54.
9 Robert McCarter, 'Escape from the Revolving Door: Architecture and the Machine', *Pamphlet Architecture*, No 12 'Building Machines', Princeton Architectural Press (New York), 1987.
10 Quoted in Robert F Marx, *Into the Deep – a History of Man's Underwater Exploration*, Van Nostrand (New York), 1989, p74.
11 CH Gibbs-Smith, *The History of Flying*, BT Batsford Ltd (London), 1953, p53.
12 Leopold Federmair, 'Verzaubern – Entzaubern' (Breaking a Spell – Casting a Spell), *Wunschmaschine – Welterfindung*, p236.
13 In his introduction to *Scheerbart's Glass Architecture*, Praeger Publishers (New York), 1972, Dennis Sharp cites Archigram's 'instant city' as a translation of this notion by a future generation.
14 Ulrich Conrads, 'Lectures on the Equilibrium. Aerial Pleasures at Around 1920', *DAIDALOS, Architecture Art Culture*, Bertlesmann-Verlag (Gütersloh), 15 September 1990, p73.
15 Speech of Privy Councillor Krummbach in Paul Scheerbart, 'Der Architektenkongress', *Frühlich* No1 (Berlin), Autumn, 1921.
16 Bruno Taut, *Die Auflösung der Städte* (The Disintegration of Cities), Folkwang-Verlag (Hagen), 1920.
17 Boris I Arvatov quoted by Milka Blizankov, 'The Materialised Utopia', in William C Brunfield, *Reshaping Russian Architecture – Western Technology, Utopian Dreams*, Woodrow Wilson Center Series, Cambridge University Press (Cambridge, Mass), 1990, p145.
18 Blizankov in Brunfield p145.
19 Nikolai Ladovski quoted by Blizankov in Brunfield, p145.
20 Selim Khan-Magomedov, *Pioneers of Soviet Architecture*, Thames & Hudson (London), 1987, p283.
21 Fritz Wichert, 'Luftschiffahrt und Architekten', *Frankfurter Zeitung*, 21 March 1909.
22 Rainer Stommer, 'The Dream of Flying Cities', *DAIDALOS, Architecture Art Culture*, Bertelsmann-Verlag (Gütersloh), 15 September 1990, pp60-64.
23 Dieter Bogner, *Haus-Rucker-Co, Denkräume – Stadträume 1967 – 1992*, Ritter Verlag (Klagenfurt), 1992, p73.
24 Wolfgang Welsch, *Aesthetisches Denken*, Reclam Jun. GmbH & Co (Stuttgart), 1990, p213.
25 Charles Jencks, 'The Architecture of the Jumping Universe', Academy Editions (London), 1995.
26 Ibid, p34.
27 W Welsch p213.
28 Published in Michael Benedikt, *Cyberspace: first steps*, Massachusetts Institute of Technology (Mass), 1991, p251.
29 Greg Lynn, 'An Advanced Form of Movement', *Architectural Design*, No 127, Academy Editions (London), 1997, p55.
30 Van Berkel, 'Yes, but. . .', *Anybody*, Cynthia Davidson (ed), conference cat, 'Anybody', Buenos Aires, June 1997, Anyone Corporation (New York), p258.
31 Lebbeus Woods, *Anarchitecture: Architecture is a Political Act*, Architectural Monographs No 22, Academy Editions (London), 1992, p40.
32 Ibid p64.
33 M Novak in M Benedikt, op cit.
34 Christian W Thomsen, *Visionary Architecture*, Prestel Verlag (Munich/New York), 1994, p156.

AT&T Global Olympic Village, 1996

FTL
AT&T GLOBAL OLYMPIC PAVILION
Atlanta

Large international events have always required temporary facilities. Recently however, higher expectations and more complex strategic ambitions have meant that events such as the Olympic Games demand infrastructural arrangements that are equal in complexity to permanent urban layouts. City-sized roads, pedestrian routes and servicing arrangements are needed to cater for the vast complexes of temporary buildings, fulfilling all the functions found in a permanent urban neighbourhood. Despite the scale of the demands, facilities must be established in a remarkably short period and, if the project is to be both economically viable and ecologically aware, should not waste rsources by being based in permanent buildings that will become redundant once the event is over.

The athletic venues and related amenities for the Atlanta Olympics were resourced in three ways: approximately a third was made up of existing local sports facilities; a second third was accommodated in new permanent constructions and the final third (about 150,000 square metres) utilised temporary and relocatable buildings and interior adaptations. FTL was one of the key design firms involved in planning the temporary infrastructure of the 1996 Olympic Games at Atlanta. They adopted several different roles during the design and implementation process: their work ranged from comprehensive organisational tasks, such as planning a range of temporary hospitality villages around the city, to specific construction projects, such as engineering the 40-metre-tall 'pyramid' structures at the Athlete's Village. Todd Dalland's experience of organising large multi-facility events, such as the Seventh on 6th Fashion Village shows at New York's Bryant Park, proved invaluable in determining the requirements of the temporary infrastructure and in urban planning.

FTL were co-designers of the 'Look of the Games', a portable kit of parts, which was used in many of the 40 separate venues as a unifying feature to help direct the hundreds of thousands of athletes and visitors. These urban-scale temporary structures were made from standard rentable items such as scaffolding with additional, specially designed modular elements, including printed-fabric panels, tensile membranes and above-ground concrete ballasting.

As project architects for the 21-acre Olympic Centennial Park, FTL provided a focus in the heart of downtown Atlanta for all the athletes and visitors. This free facility attracted crowds of up to 250,000 people and contained several venues that were open to the public long into the night. The Centennial Park's major facility was the AT&T Global Olympic Village, a 9,000-square-metre complex, comprising three relocatable buildings, which included FTL's Cadillac Exceleration Centre.

These buildings, designed in collaboration with Last Design Company, incorporated two-storey, movable-glass curtain walls, relocatable interior elevators and a second-storey bridge between buildings. This structure's fabric also became an entertainment effect in itself when images from Olympic events and live concerts were projected onto the outside of the building. AT&T plans to tour this facility, taking it first to Nagano, Japan, and then on to Sydney, Australia, for use at the Olympics in 2000.

This temporary city, enlivened by interactive communications and human activity, was constantly active during its limited life. An integral part of the design concept, however, was that it could then be dismantled and reassembled in a different form at another geographical location. In this way, it is a potent realisation of the dreams of architectural activists of the 60s and a stimulating glimpse of what a future urban environment might be like.

FROM ABOVE: Bryant Park Fashion Tent; Solar-Powered Tensile Pavilion, Nicholas Goldsmith/FTL Happold, New York; Glass Pavilion with integrated photovoltaics, Gregory Kiss & Cathcart, New York

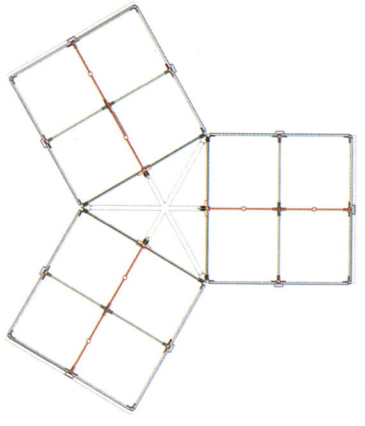

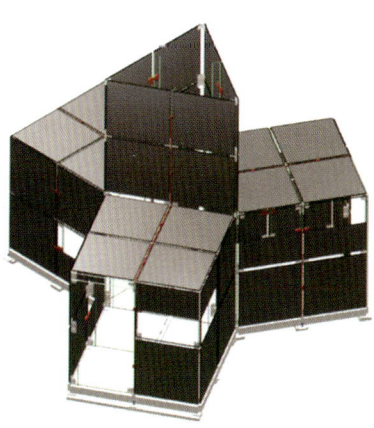

OPPOSITE FROM ABOVE: Plan of Glass Pavilion; Under the Sun, perspective view; LEFT Axonometric of Glass Pavilion

KOLATAN/MACDONALD STUDIO
TAKE 5 ON MANHATTAN
FIFTH AVENUE, NEW YORK

In 1997, the Municipal Art Society (MAS) asked ten firms of architects, artists, and landscape architects, including Kolatan/MacDonald Studio, to submit urban design proposals and strategies for Fifth Avenue, Manhattan. The resulting schemes were presented and discussed with the developers, institutions, committees and city administration who would be involved in the eventual redevelopment of this part of New York. An exhibition of the work took place at MAS' midtown premises.

In place of strategies of unilinear continuity along Fifth Avenue, Kolatan/MacDonald proposed a network model based on the notions of hybrid identities, 'co-sitation' and 'soft site'. The concept of co-sitation allows for the construction of relationships between non-adjacent sites, and the expansion of Fifth Avenue's identity, not only along its own spine, but also elsewhere in Manhattan, in a similar way to the differentiations between Broadway, Off-Broadway and Off-Off Broadway.

Thus considered, Fifth Avenue's identity is exported outwards, while other identities are imported. Sites on Fifth Avenue are termed 'soft' if both of the following criteria are present: the site is underbuilt according to the New York Zoning Ordinance; the site's Fifth Avenue identity is already infused with hybrid elements. The concept of soft site is proposed as a tactical means of accommodation. The existing buildings are incorporated into a malleable infrastructure that, by its ability to adjust and adapt to varying conditions, either avoids them entirely or merges with their different heights and building perimeters.

Manhattan's horizontal public terrain is limited. Aerial views indicate that the mid-air roofscape constitutes a second urban datum. The proposal speculates on the potential for this datum to be occupied horizontally.

Since Fifth Avenue contains only sporadic soft sites and is relatively built-up to maximum FAR in most areas (15 midtown, 10 downtown, 7 in Harlem), Kolatan/MacDonald propose to build out these air-locked areas by expanding horizontally, using transferred 'air reservoirs' from the NYP Library, the Frick Museum and St Patrick's Cathedral, and establishing foothold positions on the ground and connection to existing rooftops and elevators in the air. This would avoid the vertically extruded narrow footprint that is a result of existing development procedures.

FROM ABOVE: Computer Models: Collage lower midtown; collage Harlem proposal, towards south; Recreational fields, expanded office space

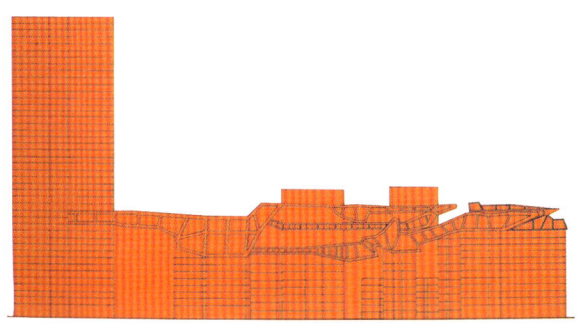

Sample Soft Site, Ground: The Harlem Block

Here, the spatial structures inhabit the ground; their co-dependencies and co-evolutions are with the streets as horizontal infrastructure rather than with the vertical infrastructures of the elevators in midtown. Therefore, their constituencies depend on accessibility of street and sidewalk. High technology and film are but two industries that can make use of large, nearly full-block floorplates in all situations, while offices, residences or live/work, as well as parking, sports facilities, commercial venues, theatres, cinema, and the like can inhabit peripheral territories including courtyard areas.

Sample Soft Site, Air: The Extended Midtown Block (23 to 59 streets)

The soft-site concept allows the development of mid-level neighbourhoods programmatically and formally by producing new relations between buildings in the same block and across blocks. The buildings are no longer only related by street locations. Furthermore, the concept permits the improvement of obsolete office buildings with small floor plates by providing an opportunity to enlarge the floors through horizontal expansion. The new structures tie into existing vertical infrastructures where desirable, but use the opportunity to connect directly to the ground through vertical footholds, which come with their own new infrastructure wherever a small building can be replaced.

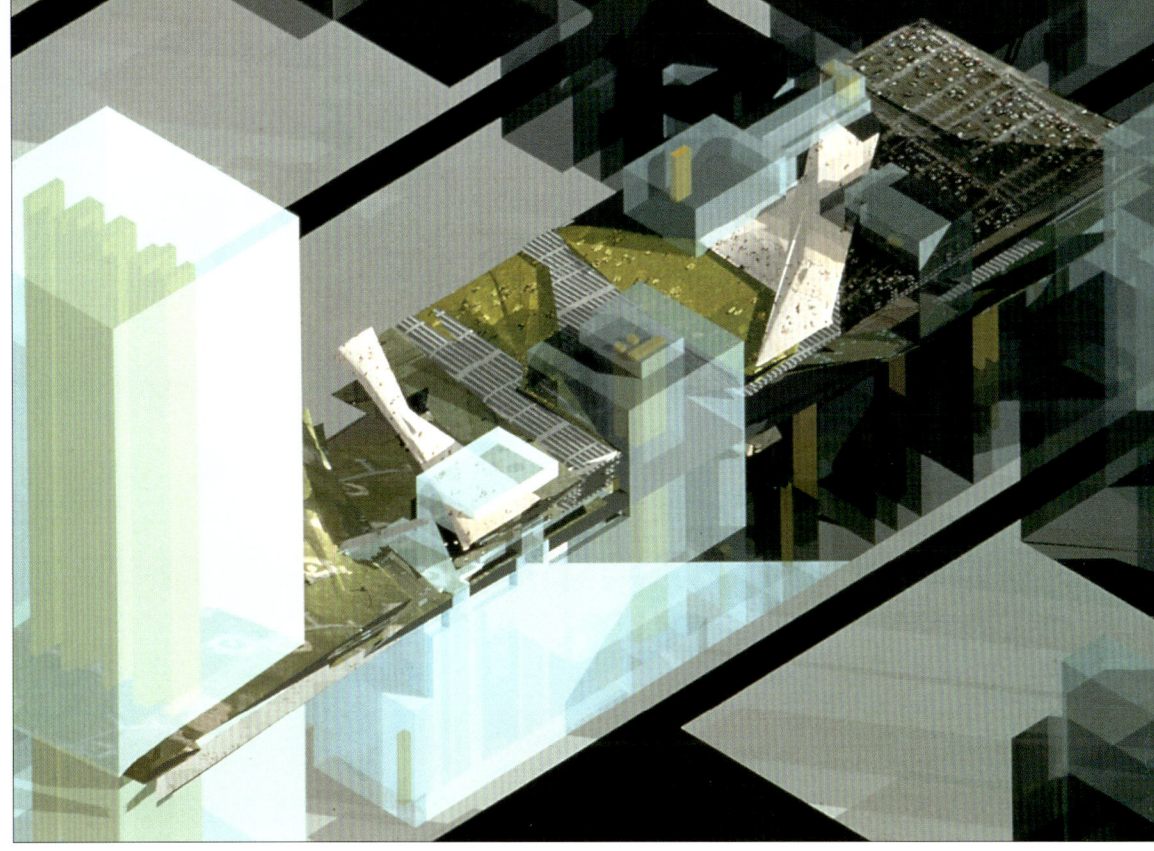

FROM ABOVE: Computer models: section with structure, proposed typical block; proposed typical block from Fifth Avenue to Madison Avenue; BELOW L TO R: Sample Soft Site Air, mid and lower midtown proposal; sample Soft Site Ground, Harlem proposal, towards north

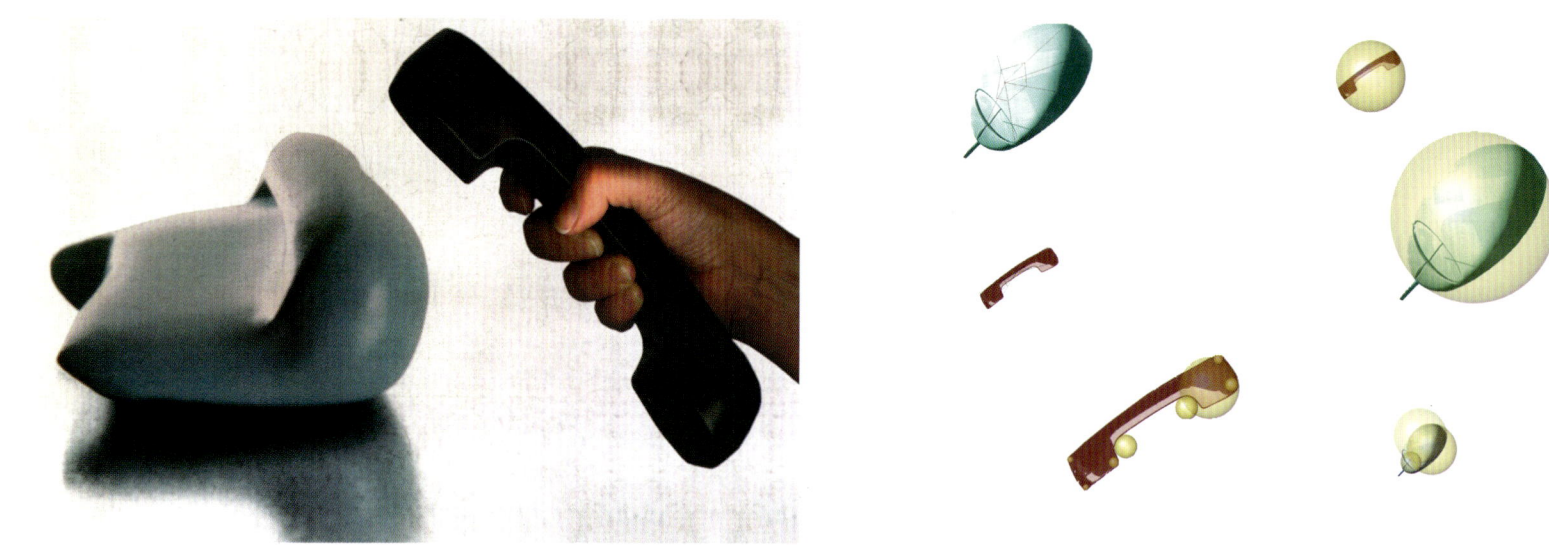

KOLATAN/MACDONALD STUDIO

VEHICLES PROJECT
San Francisco Museum of Modern Art

Eight digitally designed fibreglass vehicles were produced in sizes ranging from 3 inches to 3 feet. The moulds for the smaller pieces (up to 9 inches) were generated through stereolithography (a digitally operated, 3-D modelling technology). Those for the larger pieces were cut on CNC (Computer Numerically Controlled) machines. The finish consists of multichromatic fibreglass.

The vehicles were exhibited in 1996 in the Sandra Gering Gallery in New York. Animations of the vehicle interiors were projected onto a wall of the gallery space as a way of simulating an additional, habitable scale. The vehicles are now in the permanent collection of the San Francisco Museum of Modern Art's Architecture Department.

The problem of incommensurability has been cited as the fundamental formal problem of the 20th century. How is the relationship between a large number of very small, similar entities and a group of colossal structures built? The miniature vehicle and the gigantic spatial structure are connected programmatically through artificial protocols rather than through a container/contained relationship. What other scenarios for this miniature/gigantic interdependency can be proposed? Can the colossal structure be conceived in terms of the small entities it contains?

It is important to distinguish here between size and scale. While size denotes a quantitative material presence, scale 'is established by means of a set of correspondences to the familiar'. The extremely small, like the extremely large, turns its ordinary context into an extraordinary one. It is, as such, a vehicle of transformation of the everyday.

The vehicles are built in different sizes but are formally similar, ie, similar in quality and quantity of articulation. Rather than possessing a predetermined scale or significance, the vehicle assumes a particular scale and importance in association with many everyday contexts or in relation to some other thing or space. This is not to say that it is neutral. On the contrary, it would be more accurate to describe it as a cumulative index of multiple codes. The initial generative information was assembled from a range of existing transportation/immersion vehicles and their codes and protocols. Each new vehicle was produced from several existing vehicular morphologies (such as mouse, receiver and car seat, for example). Though the latter were selected from a multitude of scales, they were adjusted to each other in size, their particular hybridisations informed by qualitative coincidences of volume and surface articulation.

The potential programmatic appropriation of these new vehicles, their new identity as it were, would be influenced in part by their performance value at varying scales and within different scenarios and interrelations of spaces and objects.

One such possible scenario is constructed in the smaller room of the gallery. Here, the vehicle is presented to the visitor as a small object on a table and a projected architectural interior (in reference to which the object could also be regarded as a 'model'). The same set appears to the eye of the camera as a considerably larger object, sitting on what seems to be ground merging into the projected space.

In addition, there are other spatial layers to and from the exhibition web site, as well as to the stage set, all of which converge into an extended feedback system.

The vehicle is a player's item, a user's item and a collector's item. In operating in the capacity of varying agencies it is simultaneously toy, prop, instrument, object and space.

ABOVE AND OPPOSITE: Objects from the Vehicles Project

TAKASAKI MASAHARU

NANOHANAKAN – COMMUNITY CENTRE FOR SENIORS
Kagoshima Prefecture, Japan

In response to the ever-increasing number of older people in Japan today, the Prefecture of Kagoshima wished to build a 'cheerful activity centre for seniors'. Its purpose was to establish an environment in which senior citizens could create new life styles through contact and communication with other generations, either living in the local area or visiting. It would also provide health care and sports activities, including a gymnasium and rambling and jogging courses, plus facilities for craft, poetry, music, cooking, painting and shopping.

The architecture therefore needed to facilitate a flow of communication between users. Masaharu began by studying the life-style and philosophy of an older generation, with a view to adapting elements of this culture into systems of communication. The result was a space in which many different facilites and programmes interconnected, but could also operate independently of each other.

In order to encourage socialising, Masaharu devised a basic 'traffic course'

or circuit, around which patrons could circulate. Facilites connect one building to another and inside to outside in the most flexible way possible, with a central junction of all spaces forming the hub of the complex.

Crucial to the design was the fundamental idea that architectural space influences behaviour and that designing architecture is human and spiritual work. Functional design and aesthetics were evenly balanced to create a flexible area in which people would be inspired to communicate and collaborate.

The architecture evokes the climate, history and topography of Kagoshima, a mountainous area facing the southern ocean. The corridors, for example, are modelled on the Osumi and Satsumi peninsulas; the hot-spring pool and bath relates to Kirihima mountain, while the central hall suggests Kaimondake mountain. The outdoor stage represents the Satsunan islands and the grass plaza, Kinko-wan bay. The field over the grass plaza emulates the East China Sea.

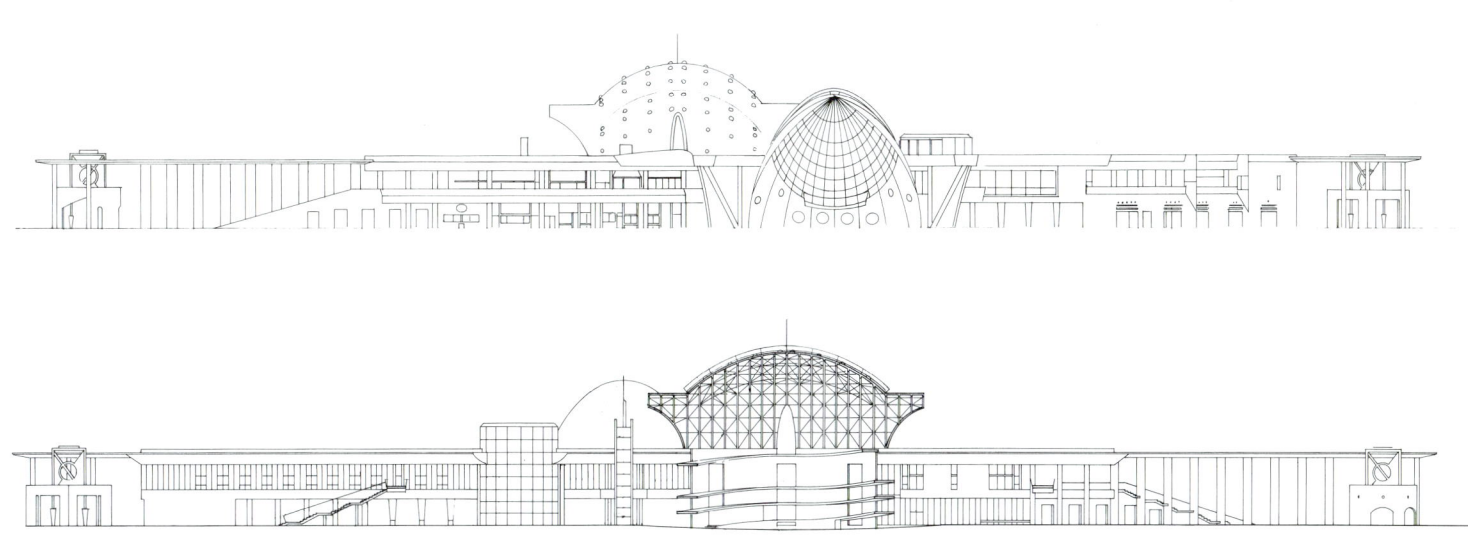

FROM ABOVE: South elevation; Section

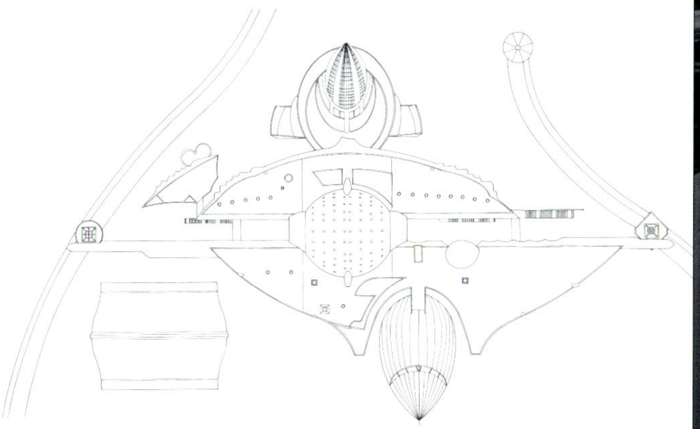

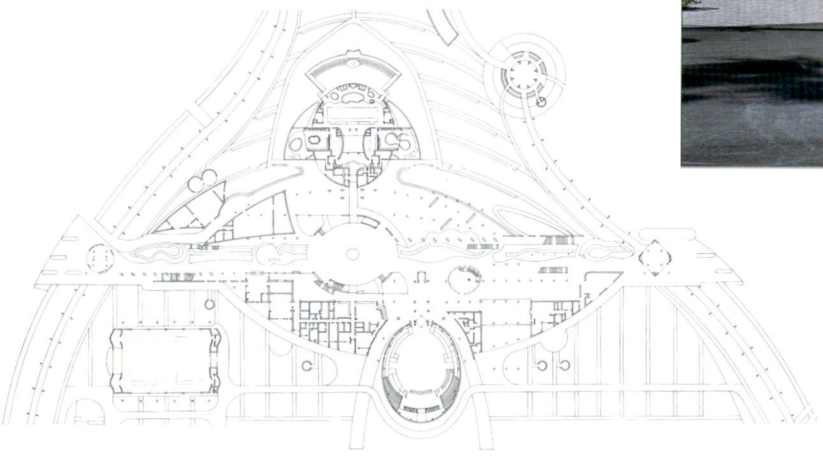

FROM ABOVE: Third, second and first floor plan

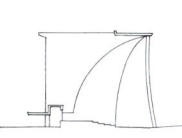

Section

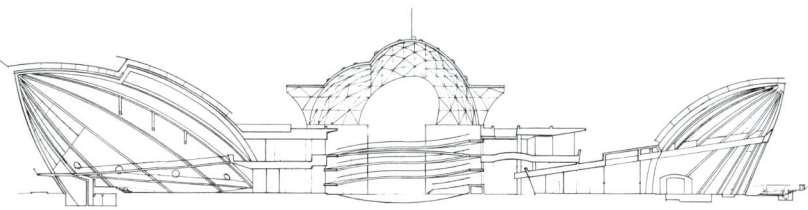

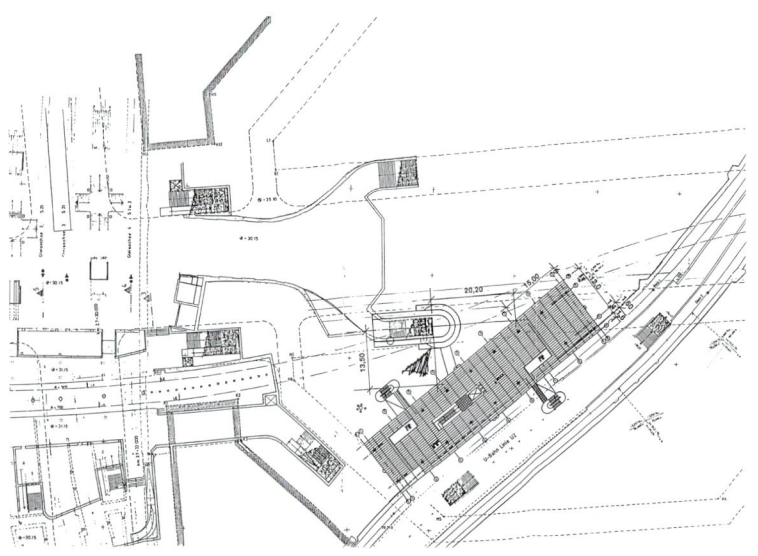

SCHNEIDER & SCHUMACHER

INFO-BOX

Berlin

In October 1994 Schneider & Schumacher was invited to participate in a competition for an information-pavilion on Leipziger/Potsdamer Platz in Berlin. The aim of the competition was to find a design that would respond to the world-wide interest in the crucial architectural changes taking place in the reunited city. The information-pavilion was aimed at the general public as well as those directly affected by the transformations in this part of the city. It was to offer a complete survey of all projects, whether financed by private enterprise or public authorities.

The goal was to produce a temporary building, whose singularity would form a clear contrast to those planned for the surrounding area. In view of the fact that for the next five years the building site would present itself to the public as an incomprehensible visual chaos of cranes and scaffolding, it seemed necessary to make a clear and unmistakable statement with the info-pavilion.

In close co-operation with the Tragwerkplanungsburo Bollinger + Grohmann (structural engineering), with whom the practice had collaborated on former projects, various structural alternatives were developed. The extremely short construction time of three months necessitated a prefabricated steel-concrete compound construction. Numerous models and 3-D animations were developed in order to ascertain exactly how many parts would be necessary and how they would fit together. In accordance with the specific task of designing a pavilion for a building site, the system of construction, and consequently the details, were kept 'rough'. This contribution to the competition received first prize and further planning took place in early 1995; the interior design was undertaken by the companies themselves.

Due to the enormous time pressure, which brought together architecture, structural engineering, and in-house technology as a whole in a very short period, the focus was placed on three main ideas: the Info-Box would 'float' exceptionally high over the ground; it would be brilliant red in colour; it would feature unorthodox 'around-the-corner' glazing.

The structure was also planned to accommodate the possibility of dismantling and reconstruction elsewhere.

Concrete-filled, steel posts of 40 centimetres in diameter form the base of the box, stabilised by diagonals across the long side of the construction, with three further diagonals perpendicular to it. The bottom platform floats 7 metres off the ground. Double-T-beams, 50 centimetres in height and 14.5 metres in length, connect the posts over a distance of 9 metres. The beams lying between the main construction are 30 cm high. The building is 62.5 metres long, 15 metres wide and 13 metres high.

All sides are covered with weatherproof panels of red steel, 2.5 x 0.5 metres in area; these serve as weather protection and thermal insulation. The glass facades, which cannot be opened, are of 50-millimetre pole-latch construction; the building is air-conditioned. Four large openings structure the box. Unconventionally, the glazing is over-edge, creating unusual views into, and even through, the structure. After encountering a breezy steel-staircase and just before entering the building, the visitor arrives at a loggia, which provides a view of the Reichstag and the area in which the Wall used to stand.

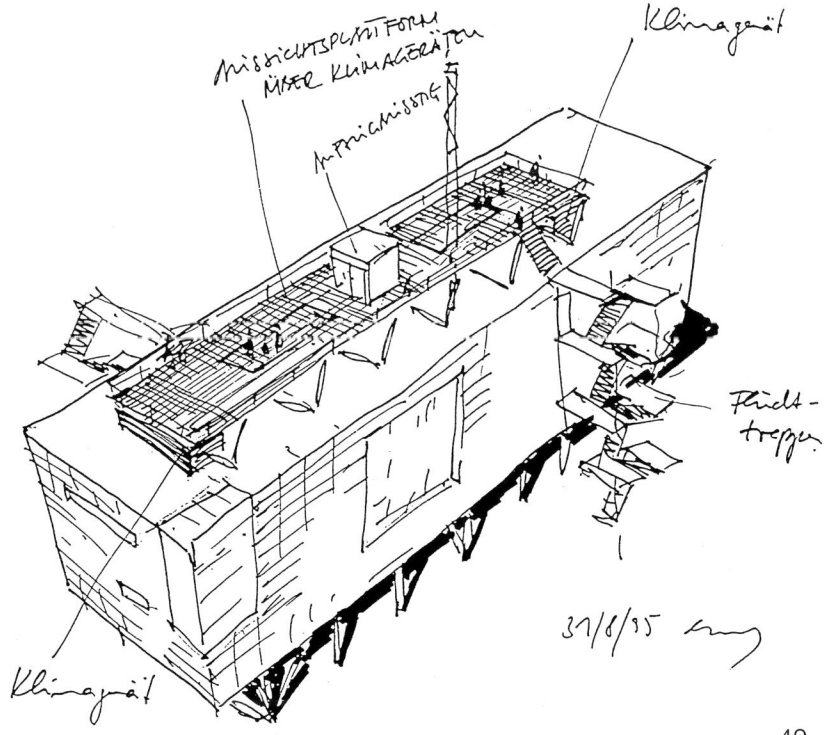

OPPOSITE: Site plan; RIGHT: Axonometric

49

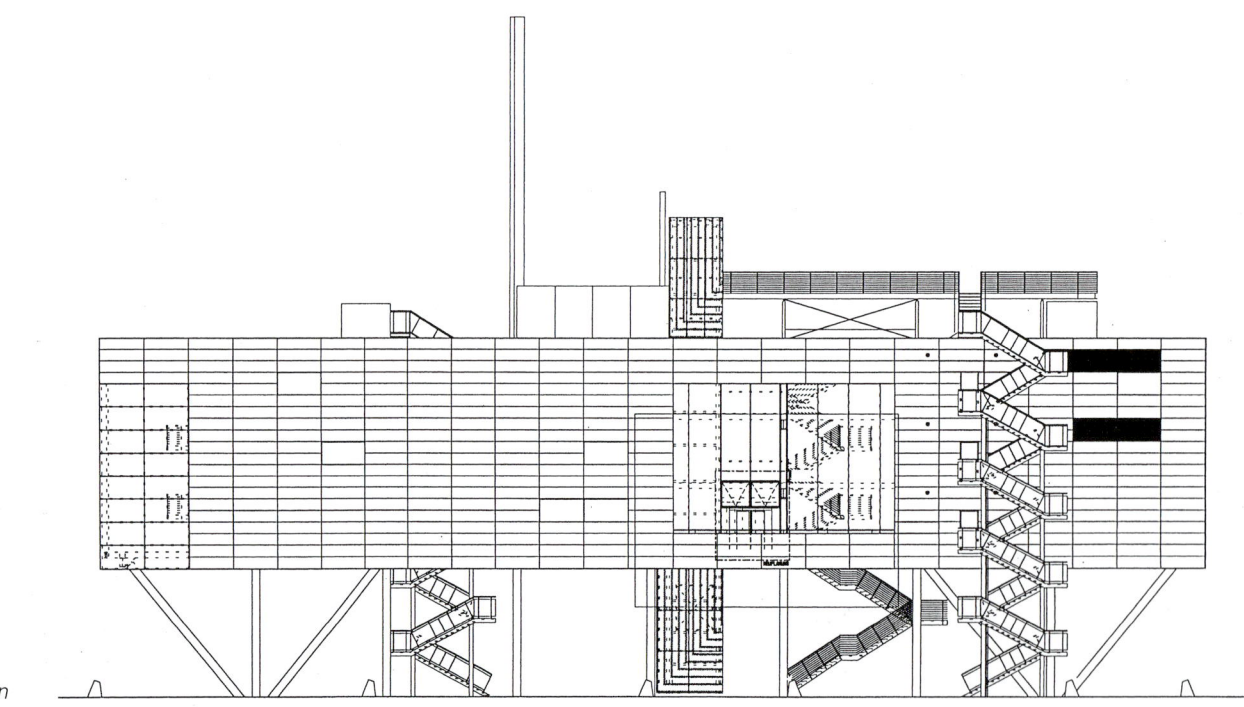

RIGHT: North elevation;
OPPOSITE: East elevation

Inside, the building is subdivided into two main parts, accessed by an entrance hall on three floors. The side facing Potsdamer Platz accommodates an assembling area, on top of which is a first-floor shopping area for souvenirs, and a top-level café with a view of the building site. The other side consists of three storeys of exhibition areas for the investors. Restrooms and sluices to the outer escape staircases can be found on each floor in both sides.

The building is accessible via a steel staircase (2.5 metres in width) as well as by an elevator, both of which are cemented in the ground level of the site. The elevator reaches up to the roof terrace (21.98 metres). The location of the house connections is underneath the entrance level. Escape ways are provided by two open steel staircases on both long sides of the building.

The inauguration took place on 16 October 1995. In 1996 the building was awarded the 'Stahlbaupreis' (Steel-building Prize) and the Berlin Architecture prize.

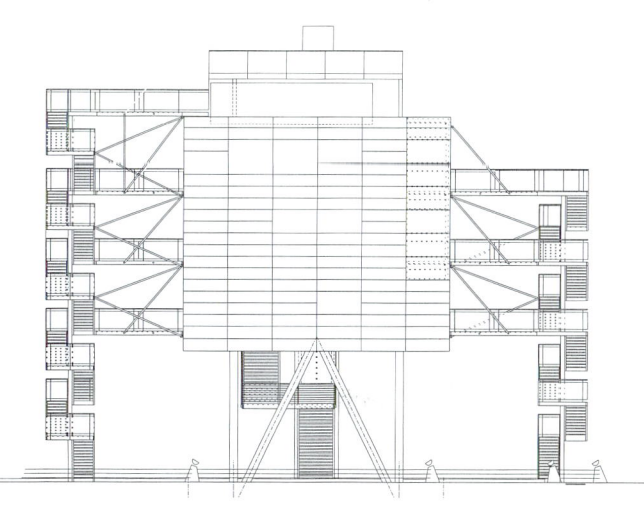

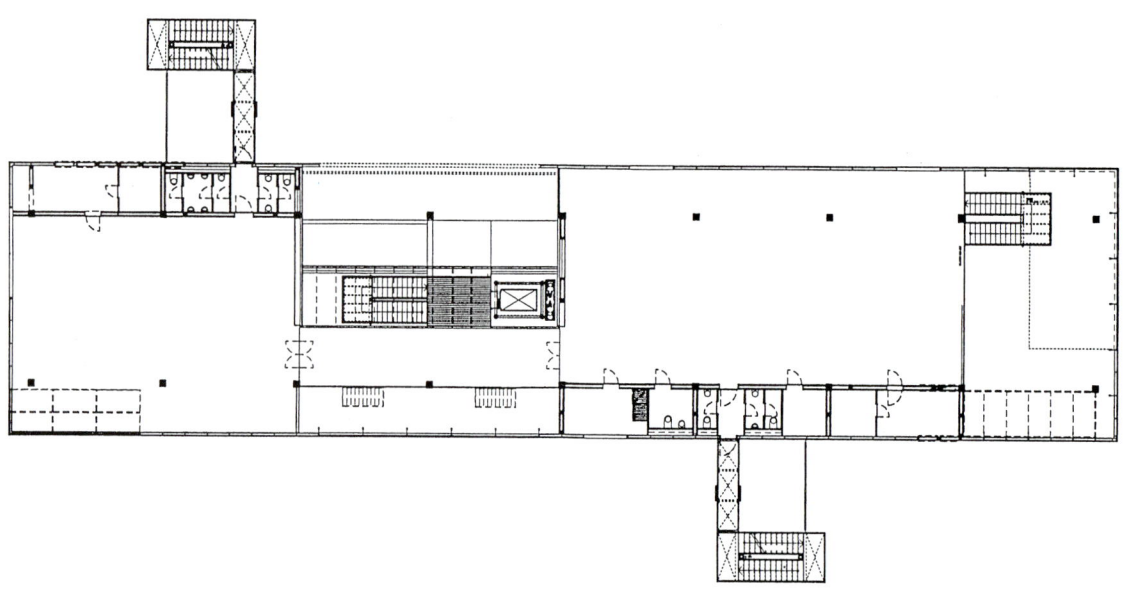

ABOVE: Third-floor plan;
BELOW: Cross section
OPPOSITE: Longitudinal section

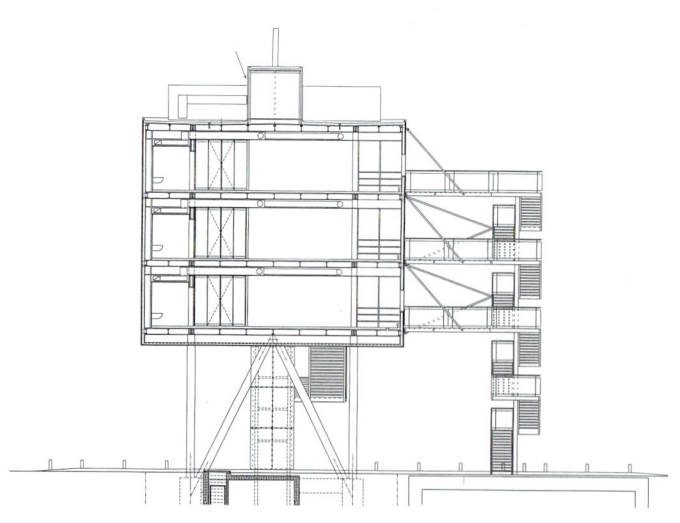

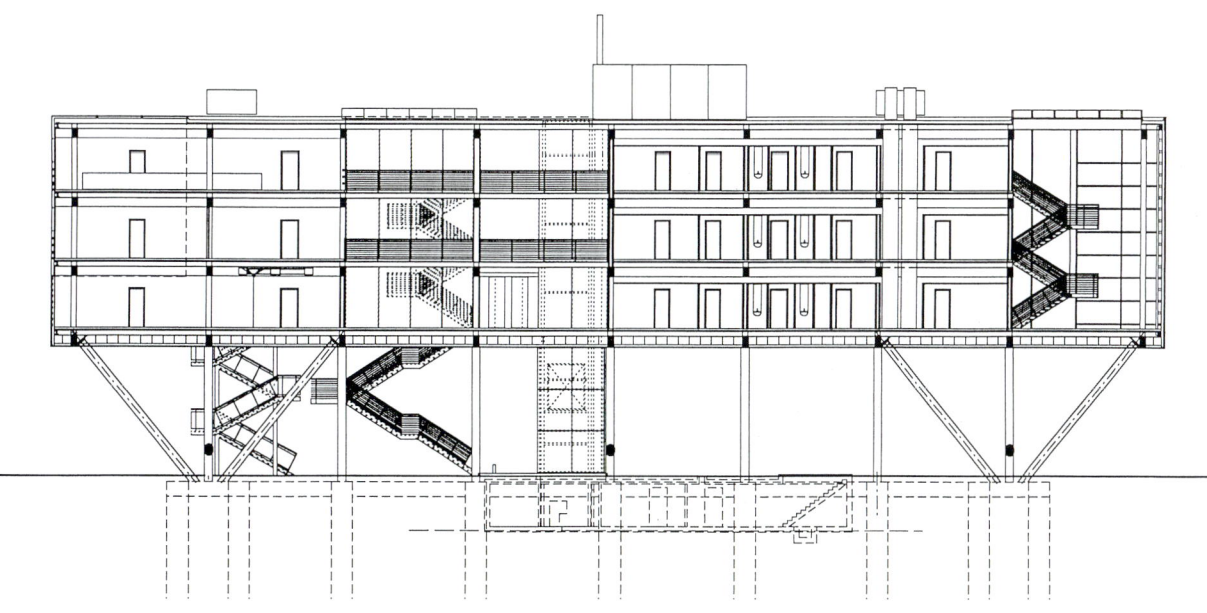

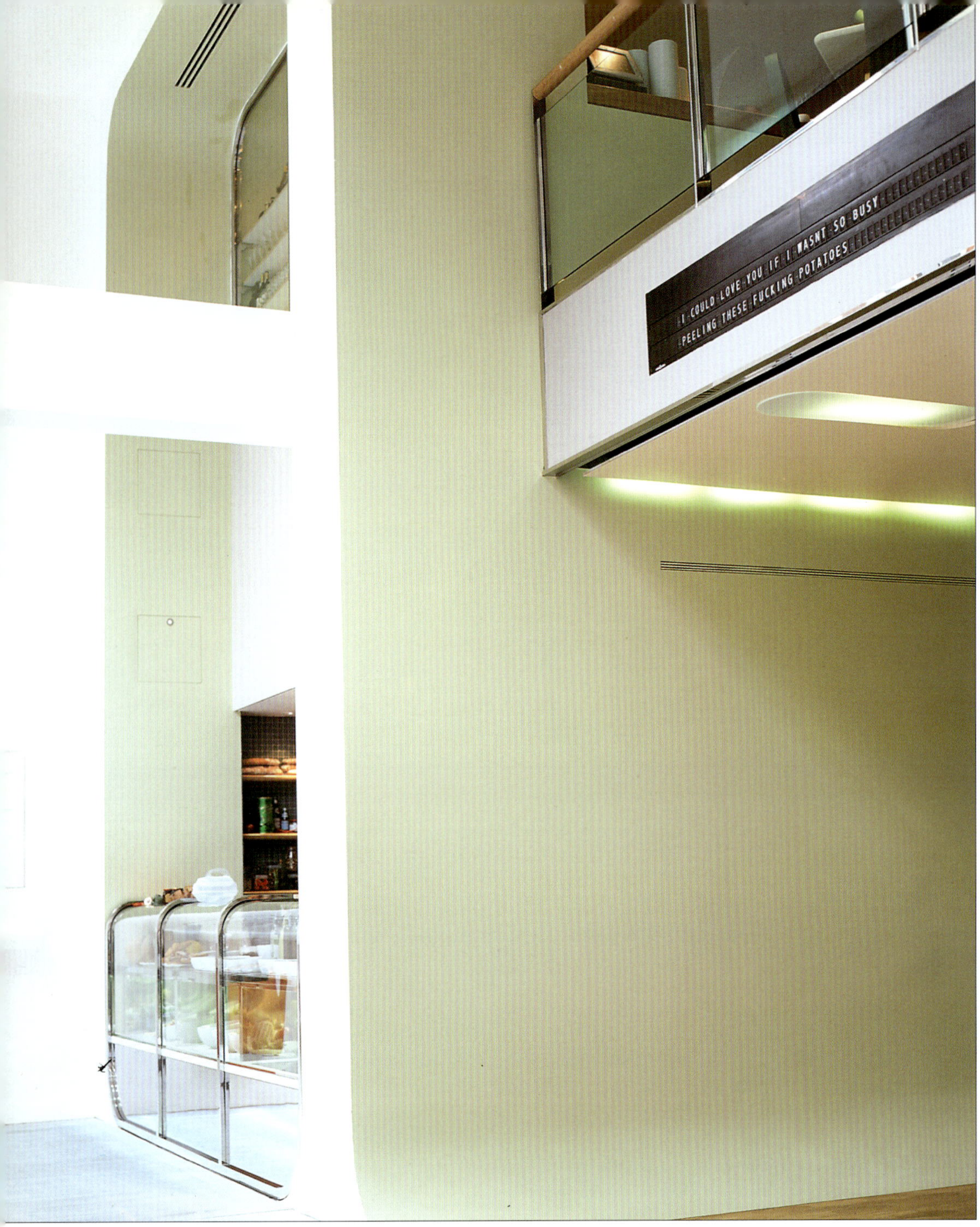
I COULD LOVE YOU IF I WASNT SO BUSY
PEELING THESE FUCKING POTATOES

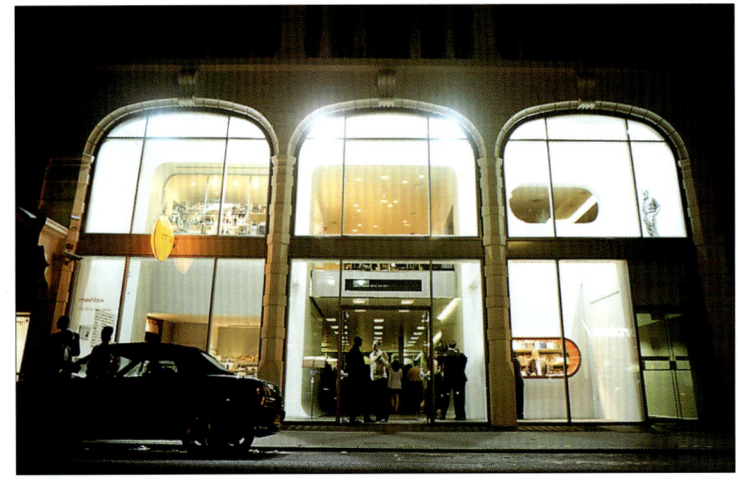

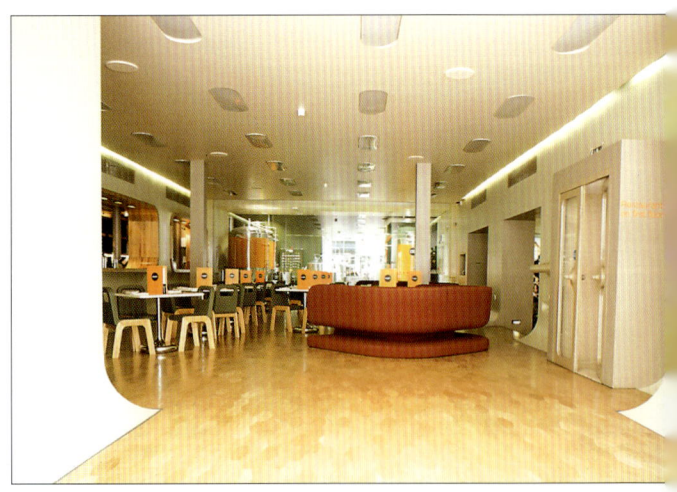

FIN
MASH 2
London

Following the flagship restaurant, Mash & Air, in Manchester, the brief for Mash 2 refined the concept into a more iconic and essential design, which would be easily transposable to future Mash sites.

Both Mash briefs called for a strong, definable architecture to emphasise the fresh operational concept of the restaurant. Mash 2, however, which was completed in 1997, was required to work within the boundaries of an existing building in Great Portland Street. This constraint helped form the idea of inserting a new architecture, with its own facade, behind the existing historical facade, juxtaposing surfaces, colours and materials.

The new insertion was to be both plastic and formal. The space was conceived by extruding a rounded polygon to create a positive space: the restaurant and bar. Contained within the resulting negative or anti-space are the auxiliary functions such as kitchens, circulation area, and further bars, which are glimpsed through openings in the skin of the positive space.

The third dimension remains strangely underdeveloped and elusive, the extrusion process being an endless repetition of a two-dimensional shape rather than the development of a three-dimensional form. The synthetic atmosphere of this two-dimensional space is informed by a computer aesthetic: forms are extruded, rotated and texture-mapped with the appropriate materials. The resulting space, with its abstraction of scale, is virtual, alien. Within this, walls and furniture become not objects, but 'thick' space.

Longitudinal section

REISER + UMEMOTO

GRAZ MUSIC THEATRE
Austria

The Music Theatre is a response to the unique programmatic, spatial and structural conditions inherent in an institution that is both educational and civic in nature. The building is comprised of two interlocking forms, each corresponding to the major programmatic functions of the institution: education and performance. The intensive daily activity of the Music College necessitates a highly functional organisation comprised of flexible, sober spaces for the development of works of music and theatre.

As such, the elements containing the academically oriented programmes operate as a kind of workshop, housed in a plinth, which receives the flow of students and faculty from the park and the college beyond. The auditorium and public spaces quite literally utilise the components of the scholastic programmes contained in the plinth as a new ground. They are accommodated within a concrete structure conceived as a forthright industrial space for the production of public events.

A long processional stair leads the public up through the body of the building, into a larger foyer and then into the main hall. At the end of an event, the audience exits via the same processional route and moves back into the city, thus completing the cycle of civic performance. While the ramp/foyer/theatre assemblage is a direct extension of the public access from Leonhardstrasse, the more academic components of the institution are aligned with the park. These are enclosed in a glass perimeter wall, providing filtered light to all of the rehearsal, changing, and production spaces. From the park, students may gain direct access to the rehearsal halls through doors located in the centre of the west facade.

The orchestra's rehearsal hall is stacked above that of the music theatre; each has a ceiling height of 4.5 metres. These spaces replicate at a reduced scale the proportions and functions of the main auditorium. They are conceived as open, flexible areas using movable seating and stage systems, which can be configured according to the needs of the directors. Both spaces benefit from light and exposure to the park. The music theatre rehearsal space is enclosed on the park side by fully operable, acoustic glass louvres, which regulate access and light. This zone operates as either a fully enclosed rehearsal hall or as a secondary foyer completely open to the park. The north walls of both rehearsal spaces and the west wall of the orchestra rehearsal space are clad on the inside with hinged, opaque panels, which open to provide natural light.

Directly adjoining the rehearsal spaces are the changing areas and ancillary functions to the music and orchestral spaces. These are arranged on three floors and connect to the rehearsal spaces via an internal circulation stair, so that the performer is never put more than a half floor from a rehearsal space. Direct access to the main auditorium is possible from all floors of the rehearsal spaces. The changing-room complex (which also includes costume and instrument storage, and offices for the Director, conductor, and visiting faculty) provides direct access to the main hall through the assembly area backstage.

Freight and passenger elevators intended primarily for performers and production uses are centrally located on the park side of the plinth, directly on axis with the service entry on Leonhardstrasse. This enables easy connections to both rehearsal spaces, the technical areas, and the auditorium. The remainder of the plinth contains the various service, technical, storage, and construction functions of both the rehearsal complex and the main hall. A mechanical room below houses electrics, plumbing, elevator lifts, and associated services.

The theatre's entry locks into the axis of the courtyard between the Palais Meran and the Remise, drawing the flow of people through the lobby (containing ticketing, coat-check stations, and

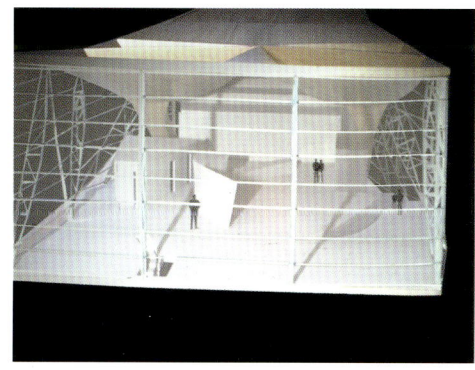

Computer-generated perspectives

restrooms) immediately up into the foyer by way of a grand staircase, beginning under the massive theatre volume and swerving outward, rising in the space between the theatre and the structure of the curtain wall overlooking the park beyond.

The foyer (containing the restaurant/cafeteria, bar and restrooms) extends across the entire north end of the building at a height of 10 metres, just inside a glass facade. It constitutes a civic space in its own right, serving the formalised rituals of theatre-going during performances in the main hall. A large expanse of open floor, surrounded by dramatic, soaring concrete and crystalline glass is thus provided. In the day-to-day activities of the college, the foyer is used for informal gathering, study, and dining at the bar/canteen. It is also suitable for a variety of large- or small-scale events.

The intense spatial effects produced by the hanging conoids above, and the cascading processional stair below, draped in the oscillating flow of the curtain wall, draws the visitor down to the main hall. The hall is essentially an empty concrete box, open to the invention of the director and performers, since seating and stage elements are entirely flexible. The backstage complex consists of a large seating assembly and storage area with direct access to the elevator core and the orchestra rehearsal space. Emergency exits, access to the control rooms and the lighting grid, and handicap access to the main hall and control rooms via elevator are all provided at the extreme south end of the building.

The Music Hall employs two different sets of construction and material systems to respond to the disparate programmatic imperatives of education and performance.

The plinth employs conventional steel-frame, glass-clad construction. With the exception of the mechanical room housed in the basement, it rests on grade to minimise the costs associated with extensive excavation. Floor plates are of composite construction, with relatively thin steel members connected to concrete slabs with studs. The plinth is clad in thermally insulated, transparent and translucent glass panels from floor to ceiling. Interior partitions are of gypsum board on steel studs. The two rehearsal spaces have increased wall thicknesses to allow for acoustic isolation. Furthermore, all glazing surrounding the rehearsal spaces is both thermally and acoustically insulated.

The concrete structure encompasses the main hall and the cantilevered double-conoidal roof over the north half of the building. The auditorium is a

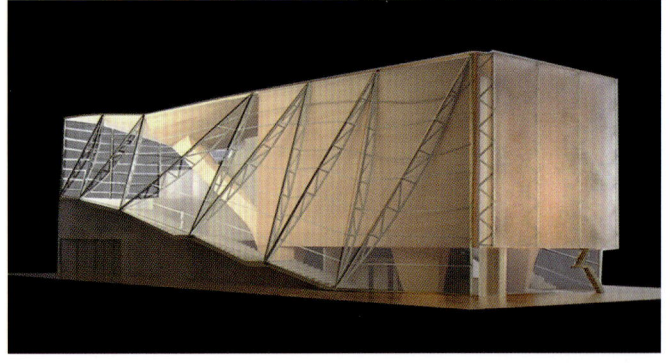

Model view from park and computer-generated exterior

reinforced-concrete box, raised 4 metres up on reinforced concrete piers. Wall thickness around the main hall is 45 centimetres to provide adequate acoustic isolation. The flat, reinforced-concrete roof of the hall is of waffle-slab construction, the coffers and beams running diagonal to the axis of the hall at a depth of 1 metre. The considerable tensile forces generated by the cantilever of the double-conoidal roof are thus transferred into the walls of the main hall, the structure of which behaves in the fashion of a massive beam. The 1-metre-deep, reinforced-concrete floor of the auditorium also handles tensile forces exerted by the cantilever.

The sculptural effect of the double-conoidal roof is belied by the simplicity and economy of its construction. The conoid is a ruled surface, obtained by sliding a straight line segment with one of its ends on a curve and the other on a straight line. Thus, the geometry of the entire form of the roof is constructed of straight lines. The double-conoid behaves as a cantilevered shell (designed for a maximum snow load of 3 metres), allowing for a dramatic span of 30 metres over the public foyer. It is constructed of spray-on concrete over formed wire-mesh, thus obviating the need for expensive form work. The compressive forces of the cantilever are transferred through two large diagonal support members into the front two piers of the concrete box, and from there into the footings below. Within the diagonal supports are drains adequate to handle all roof runoff.

The curtain wall is a system that mediates between the plinth and the concrete structure. Its main structural elements are triangulated steel-truss members, the endpoints of which connect the edges of the two systems around the building's perimeter.

On the exterior, these trusses carry a grid of lighter glazing mullions, and on the interior, a mesh of closely spaced aluminium rods to act as a sunscreen and to provide dramatic spatial definition. Truss depth is dependent upon length, the maximum depth being 1.4 metres, the minimum, 0.5 metres.

Every bow is cut from the same radius (45 metres), lending a substantial economy to their construction. The final configuration of the curtain wall is a series of large, triangular facets, which hold the exterior mullion grids, providing a flat exterior surface for glazing. The bows of each truss are oriented towards the interior of the building, giving a convex curvature to the sunscreen elements.

West elevation

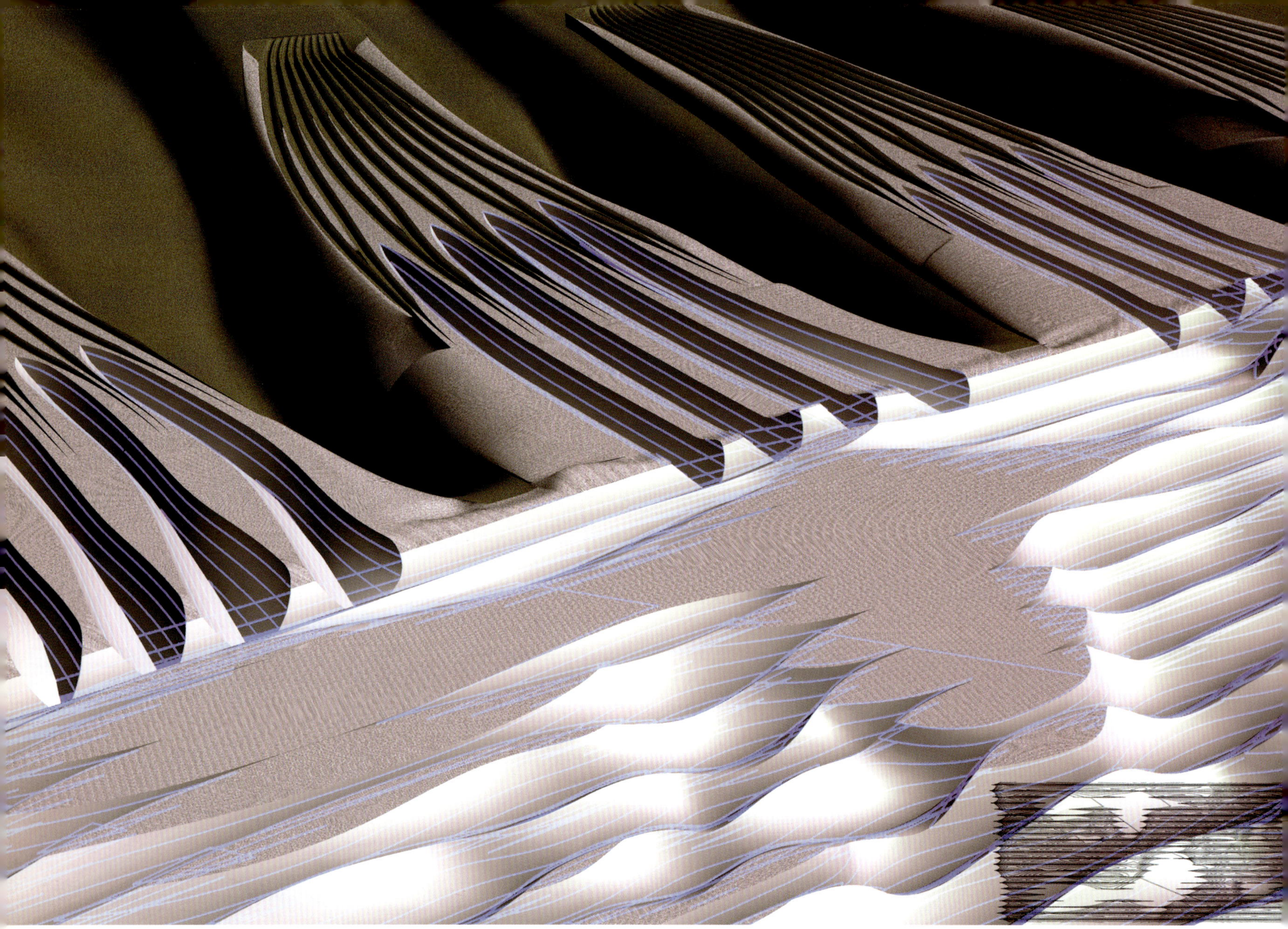

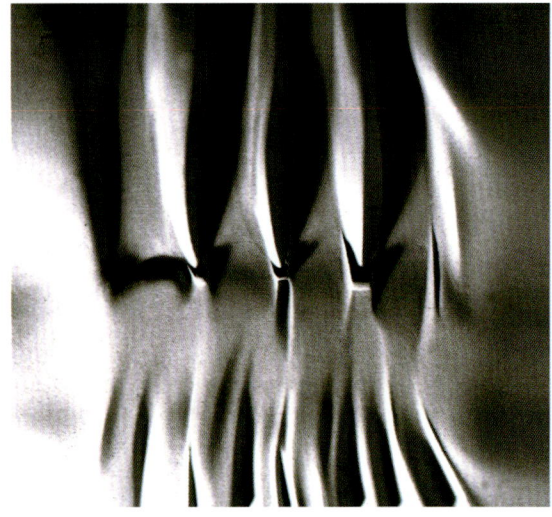

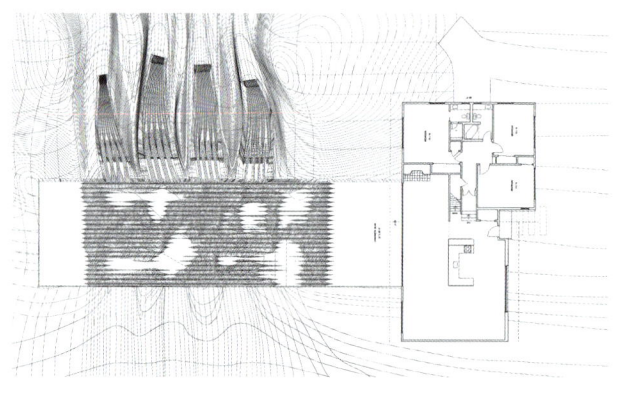

ABOVE: Oblique rendering; CENTRE: Model plan; site plan;
RIGHT: Density map of laminar system

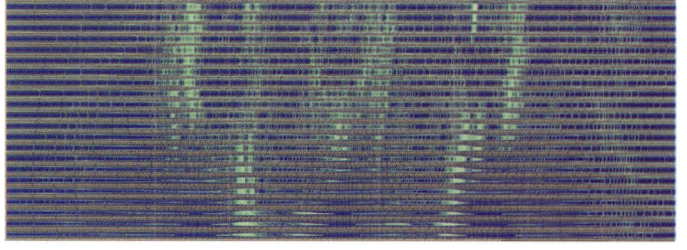

REISER + UMEMOTO
WITH DAVID RUY AND JEFFREY KIPNIS
WATER GARDEN

The architecture of the garden has historically encompassed the full range and implications of Man's engagement with the material environment. A more or less permanent feature of Western architecture has been the almost ineradicable idea that there exists a permanent and unchanging essence behind the world of appearances, that is universalised themselves in fixed, simple geometries and timeless typologies. Time thus makes itself evident within two distinct yet related schemas: first, architecture as a stable and unchanging framework within which, and against which, the temporal unfolds; and second, experimentation with how the mutable character of nature can be made to approach or deviate from a certain ideal.

In the 18th-century French topiary garden for example, the relative crudity or refinement of simple geometrical forms in plant materials served to establish the norms and limits for their speculation and enjoyment. If, however, we shift our focus from such static models of nature and architecture to dynamic (essentially time-based) systems, a new horizon of possibilities emerges. Time, reappears as something real – as a destabilising but creative milieu. That is to say, time is not understood to be prior to, above, or separate from the material world, but is engendered by, and finds its particular incarnations within it.

Nature then, is less a 'creation' on which to speculate than an inventive and modifiable matrix of materials. It might be argued that abandoning the two schemas outlined above leads to forms where nature is in some sense allowed to take its own course (with the assumption that natural development without human intervention will display its own creativity and inherent virtues). However, a fourth possibility exists, which contrary to a passive naturalism, requires intensive artifice towards the production of natural effects. Nature will of its own inertia tend towards developments of increasing stability and banality. A salient and

intensive architecture requires the deliberate production of instability in order to produce novelty. And here it will be necessary to set aside the nature/culture dialectics and focus instead on the processes that establish transverse developments across these regimes.

The French philosopher Gilles Deleuze coined the concept of the 'machinic phylum' to refer to the overall set of self-organising processes in the universe. These include all processes in which a group of previously disconnected elements (organic and inorganic) suddenly reach a critical point at which they begin to 'co-operate' to form a higher-level entity. Recent advances in experimental mathematics have shown that the onset of these processes may be described by the same mathematical model. It is as if the principles that guide the self-assembly of these machines 'are at some deep level essentially similar'. The notion of a 'machinic phylum' thus blurs the distinction between organic and non-organic life.

This material geometry constitutes the 'primitive', through which a hierarchical series of global and local transformations (warps, dimples, folds) is expressed. Extreme and unstable configurations in the topology are essentially built into the concrete substrate, materialising in the vital media (water, soil, plant materials and chemical salts) of the 'flow space' above. The topology of the substrate induces transformational events that introduce real discontinuities in the evolution of the media flowing on it. In such manifold topologies the characteristics of the mapped media are not determined by the quantitative substrate, but by the specific singularities of the 'flow space' of which it is itself part. This means that the 'dead' yet intensive geometry of the grooves excites material and/or biological novelty in the media. In literal and instrumental fashion, multiform gradients in the geometry 'diagram' trigger the gradients of growth inherent in natural systems and yield a prodigious, if only partially manageable, field of blooms.

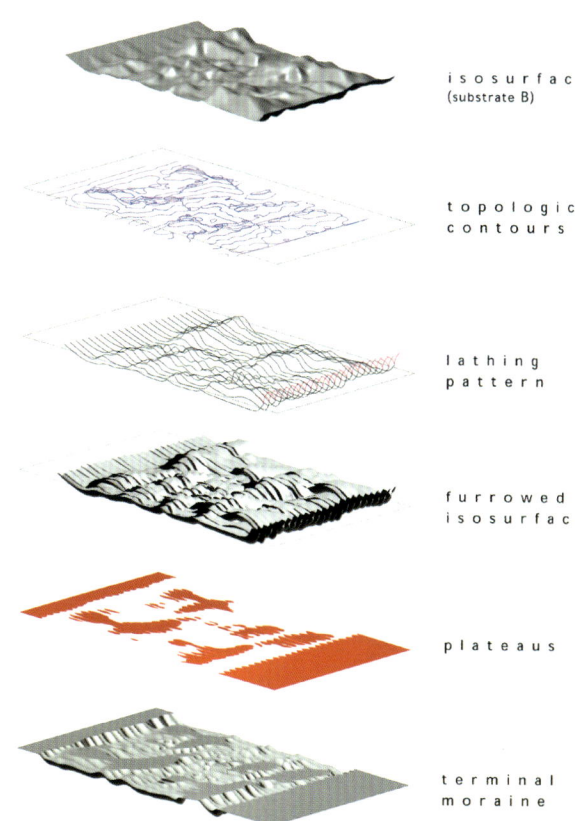

isosurface (substrate B)

topological contours

lathing pattern

furrowed isosurface

plateaus

terminal moraine

ABOVE: Isometrics; BELOW: Model

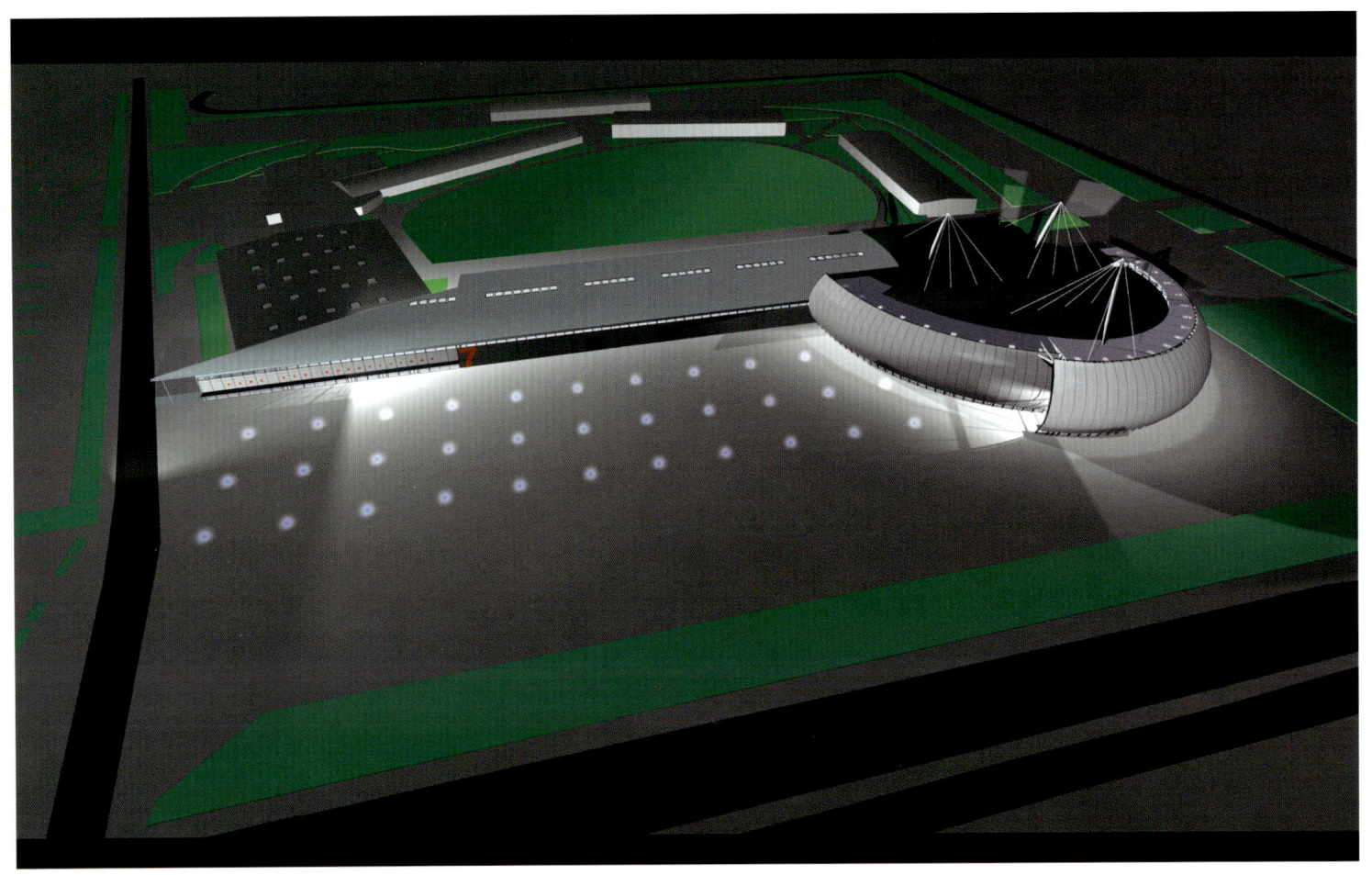

BERNARD TSCHUMI ARCHITECTS

PERFORMANCE HALL AND EXHIBITION CENTRE
Rouen, France

The crux of this project, scheduled for completion in Autumn 2000, was to create a tool capable of fostering, at the beginning of the 21st century, both the economic expansion and the cultural development of the Rouen district. The site, currently banal but ripe with potential, is well located, at the entry to Rouen, less than an hour and a half from Paris. As seen from the National Route 138, the tripartite ensemble – a 7,000-seat concert hall, an open public place, and a new 7,000-square-metre exhibition hall – aims for a strong, contemporary image, a spark for cultural and economic rebirth.

The two buildings offer a degree of polyvalence: the new exhibition hall allows a vast diversity of organisational schemes to accommodate conventions for large public crowds or trade fairs for limited groups of professionals; 220 metres in length, it is conceived as a simple structure with a slightly vaulted roof. Its overriding horizontally contrasts

with the proliferating curves and the guywired masts of the concert hall. The support points in the ceiling structure of the vault area are designed to maximise the flexibility of the exhibitions on the open floor below.

The concert hall is conceived primarily for popular music, but is proportioned to accommodate all types of musical and sporting events including political conventions, summer schools, or theatrical shows. Over 110 metres in diameter, it transforms the typology of the classic concert hall through the asymmetrical rotation of the auditorium away from the axis of symmetry of the stage.

In addition to this reduction of the strict frontality of the stage, this structure accommodates the off-centre entry condition imposed by the site and allows the theatre to be more easily reconfigured into three smaller volumes. The mast-and-guywire structural system of the roof allows both an economical long span

over the space of the concert hall, and long-distance visibility from the highway: the three masts are illuminated on concert evenings.

The necessity for acoustical isolation of the concert hall from its surroundings led to a complete double envelope. The inner skin – the concrete, stepped seating – is doubled by the exterior skin – two segments of broken, tilted *tori* made of insulated corrugated metal. The bowed, curvilinear entry hall is formed by the loose fit between these two skins.

Along its length, this programmatic and physical buffer space undergoes continuous variations to accommodate the different contingencies of circulation (access to hall and fire exits) and lobby functions (bars, box-office, etc).

The outer skin is generated by establishing describable geometries, which connect the different sectional conditions suggested by these programmes.

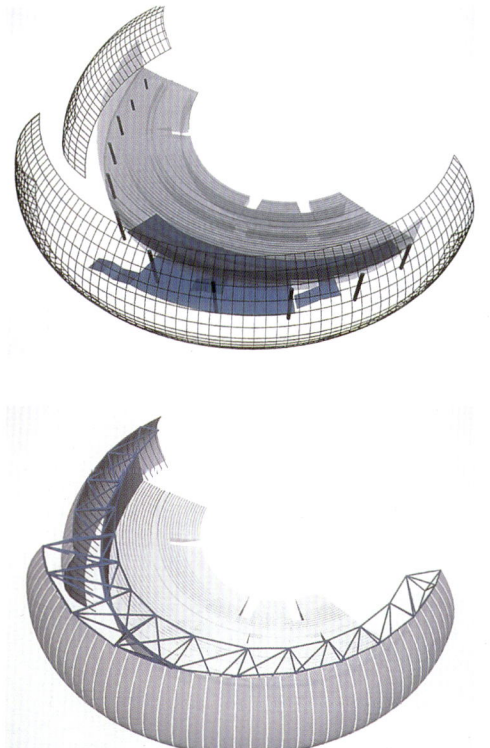

OPPOSITE FROM ABOVE: renderings of site and Concert Hall interior; ABOVE: Renderings of entry hall

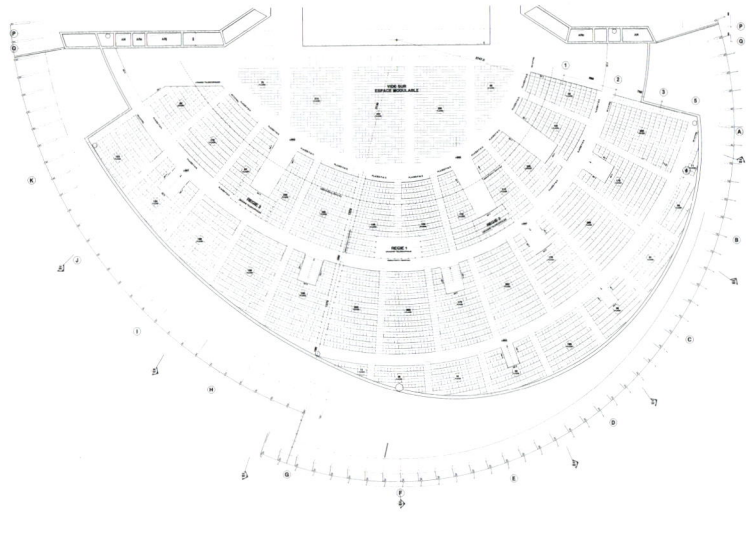

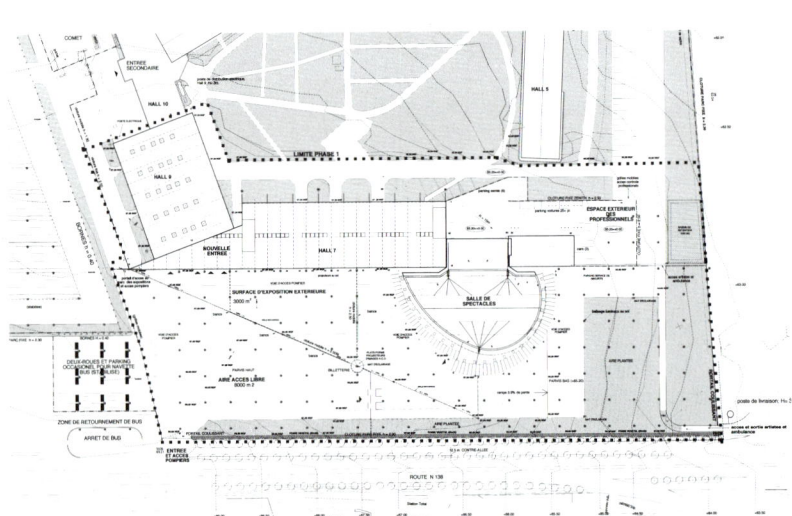

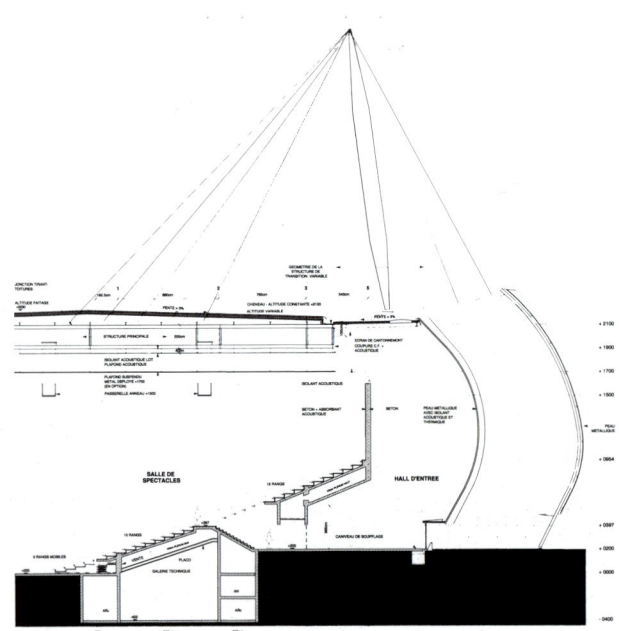

FROM ABOVE: Performance hall plan; site plan; section

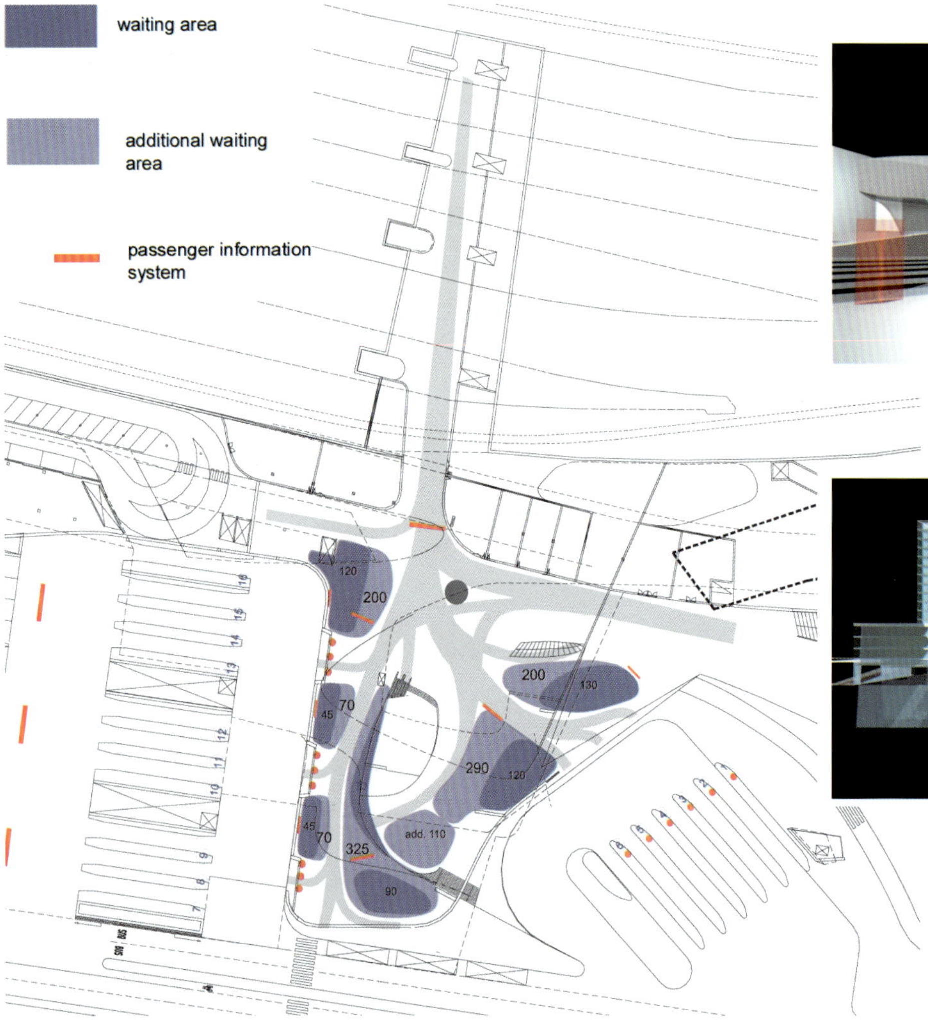

waiting area

additional waiting area

passenger information system

FROM ABOVE: Diagram showing integration of v-walls and landscape; distribution of programmatic zones; front view and longitudinal section; LEFT: Site plan

VAN BERKEL & BOS

INFRASTRUCTURAL PROJECT
Arnhem, The Netherlands

In August 1996, Van Berkel & Bos was asked by Arnhem City Council to develop a coherent plan for a new station area. The existing complex of bus terminals and the train station no longer satisfied the ambitions of the town council and the NS (Dutch Railways). The proposed plan unites infrastructural aspects and building concepts from previous studios, forming the basis for the development of a new, high-standard public space.

The revised identity of the station area acknowledges the strong regional importance of Arnhem. With its central bus-stops for regional and urban travel and the planned parking facilities, the station area forms the main entrance to the town, through which more than 65,000 people pass every day. This accentuates the need for a good connection to the shopping precinct and an improvement in the urban quality of the area in general.

In the proposal, the bus terminal and train station are combined into a new, integrated type of public transport complex. The area takes on the form of a climatised inner court that gives direct access to trains, taxis, buses, bikes, parked cars, office spaces and the town centre. The naturally sloping landscape of Arnhem allows the bringing together of all these transport systems and facilities. Natural differences in height, walking routes, sight lines and a density survey determine the position of the folds.

The intersection of different traffic systems is reduced to a minimum in order to maintain good accessibility to all the facilities. Pedestrians can find their bearings and choose their destination at a glance. This sense of orientation is enhanced by the penetration of light at essential points, such as the entrances to the station and the offices. Human movement, transport systems, light and construction are inextricably linked.

Diagram of landscape, vs and double layered roof

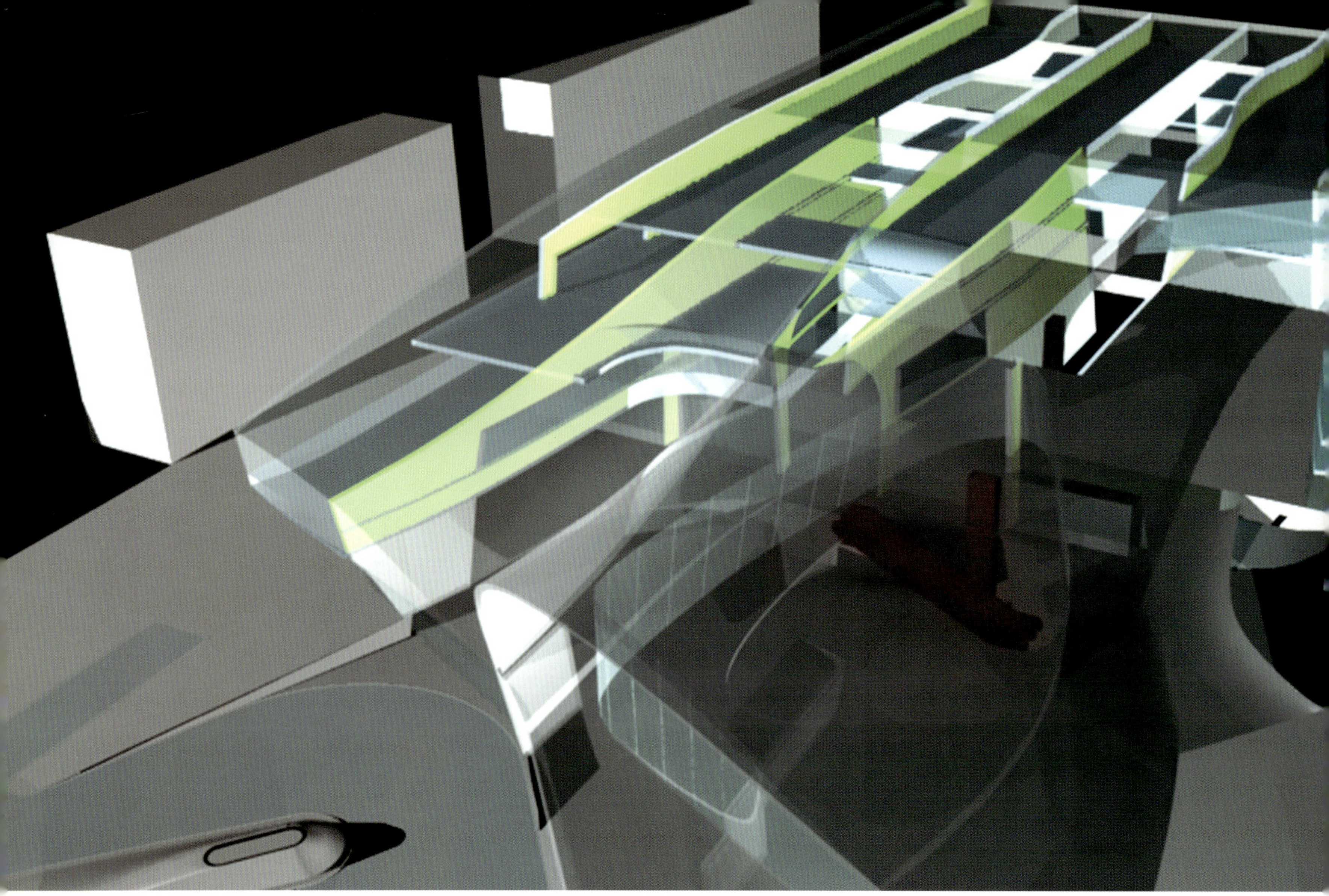

FROM ABOVE: v-walls and turning into roof of transfer hall; transfer hall view; study model

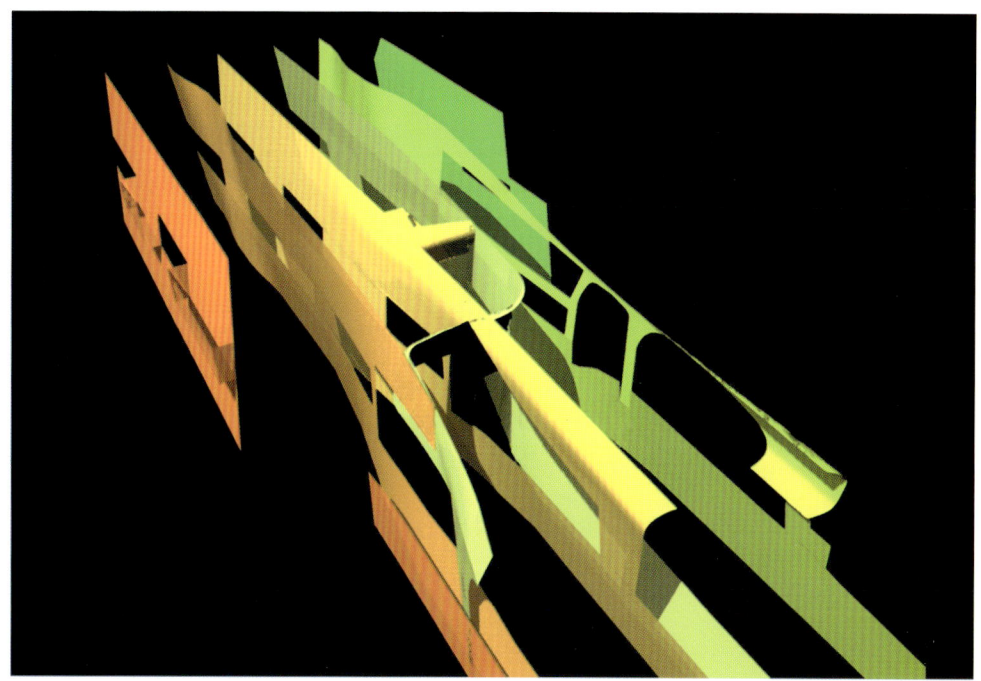

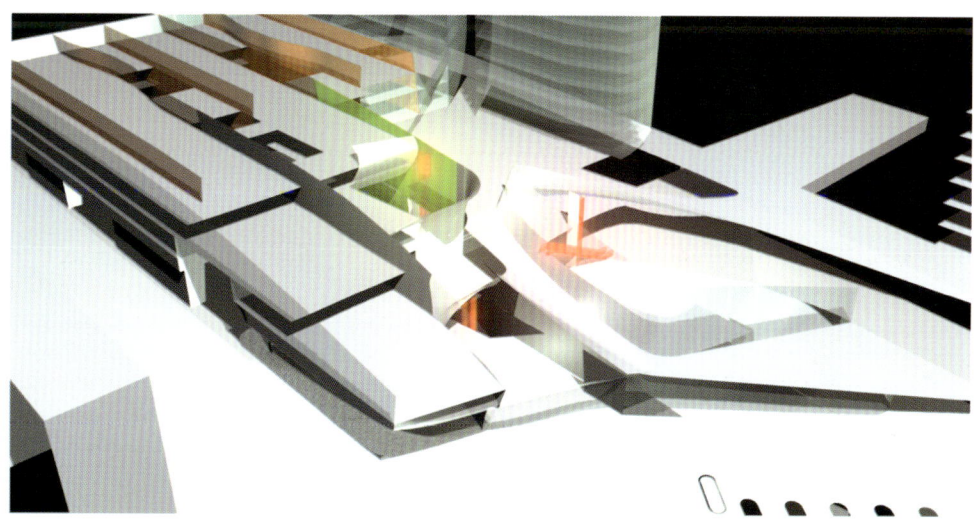

FROM ABOVE: v-shaped walls; "wormhole" connection of different levels; public connection between transfer hall, office development and city centre

COOP HIMMELB(L)AU

CLOUD #9

Geneva

The formation of Coop Himmelb(l)au in 1968 was based on the desire 'to make architecture as buoyant and changeable as clouds'. The concept for Cloud #9 goes back to these roots in order to move forward.

At the end of the 20th century, and especially in the context of a competition for the United Nations, the idea of the cloud has fresh relevance. The increasingly fuzzy socio-political structure of the world can be compared to the structure of the cloud. As a product of the complex web of influences upon it, rather than of specific intention, the cloud eludes identity. In this way, the cloud as method threatens to erode the control of the architectural designer, thereby opening up new fields of spatial possibility.

Just as the form of a cloud is sensitive to heat, wind, and air pressure, the design for the Place des Nations, Geneva, 1995, is sensitive to the forces of site and programme, to the power of the city. The space of the cloud is blown up at the intersection of urban planning parameters, height limits and circulation vectors.

The result is a soft, fluctuating enigma – a building that does not want to be a building. The envelope of the cloud becomes a glass mesh construction that loosely defines a semi-public space. The permeability of this shell allows views of the movement of people through layers of light and colour. The space becomes a crossing point for diplomats, students and tourists, as well as a gateway from the city of Geneva into the International Zone of the United Nations.

Within this envelope, private office blocks containing consulates and missions are cantilevered from concrete elevator cores.

The space between the shell and the blocks, used for balconies and ramps, precipitates passive energy gains and a cloud-like circulation of air.

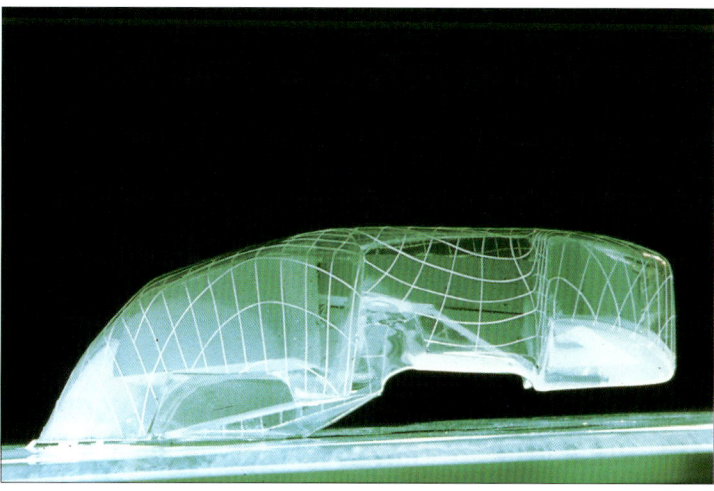
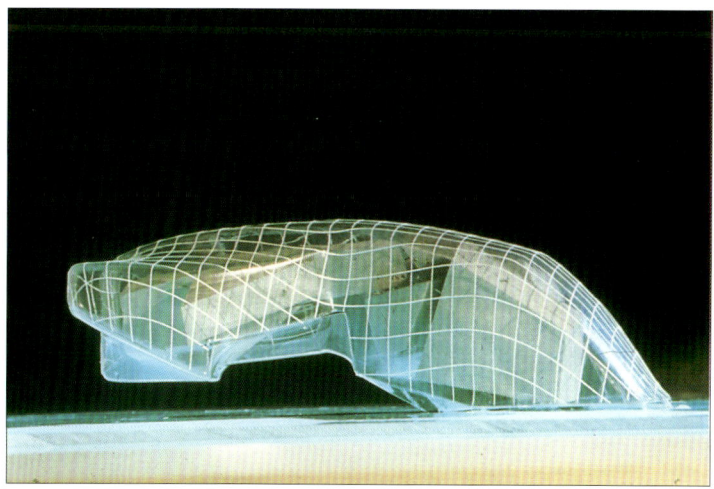

BRANSON COATES ARCHITECTURE
NATIONAL CENTRE FOR POPULAR MUSIC
Sheffield

The National Centre for Popular Music was completed in August 1998 for Music Heritage Ltd. Branson Coates liken its design to a jukebox, allowing for randomly accessible events. Situated in Sheffield's rapidly expanding cultural industries quarter, the 4,000-square-metre complex consists of four drums. These house the main elements of the exhibition programme: an interactive exhibition gallery celebrating the history and development of popular music; a practical display area exploring the mechanics of how popular music is created, recorded and distributed; a sound arena where art and technology combine to create musical environments; a gallery for temporary exhibitions.

The glazed crossing between the four drums acts as the inter-connecting public foyer and coincides with the paths of the city. Visually, the drums are reminiscent of the great industrial structures that characterise the Sheffield landscape. Each drum is clad in stainless steel and the undercut at street level is glazed to intensify the urban relationship of the cafés and shops. The cowls on top of the drums rotate slowly into the wind to provide natural, low energy ventilation.

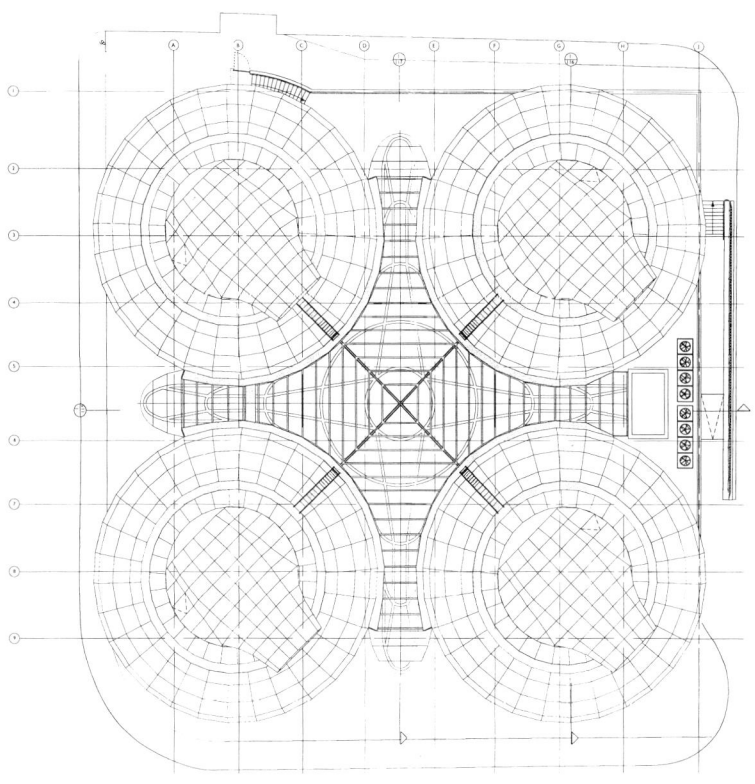

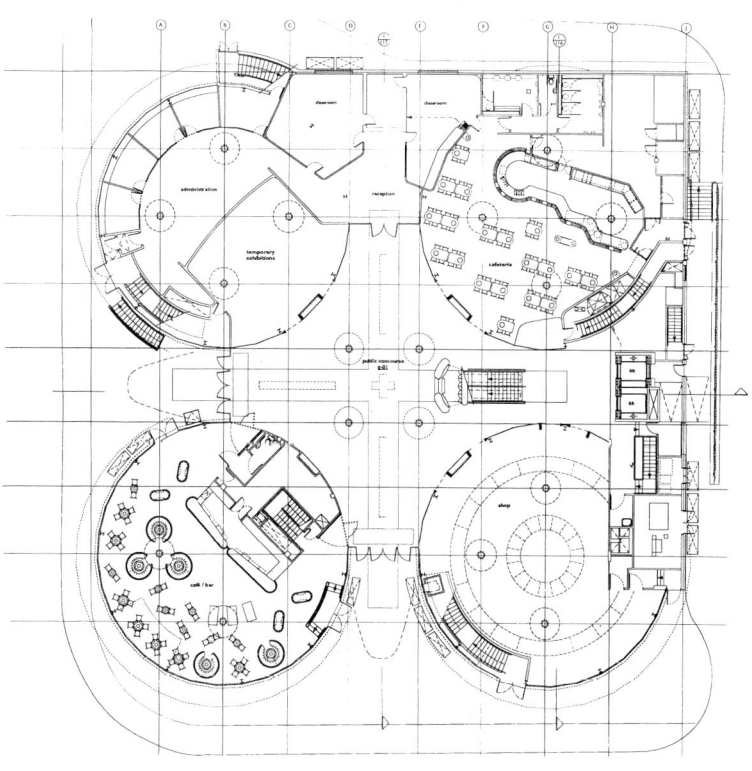

OPPOSITE: Section; FROM ABOVE: Roof plan; ground-floor plan

...a jukebox of pop experience

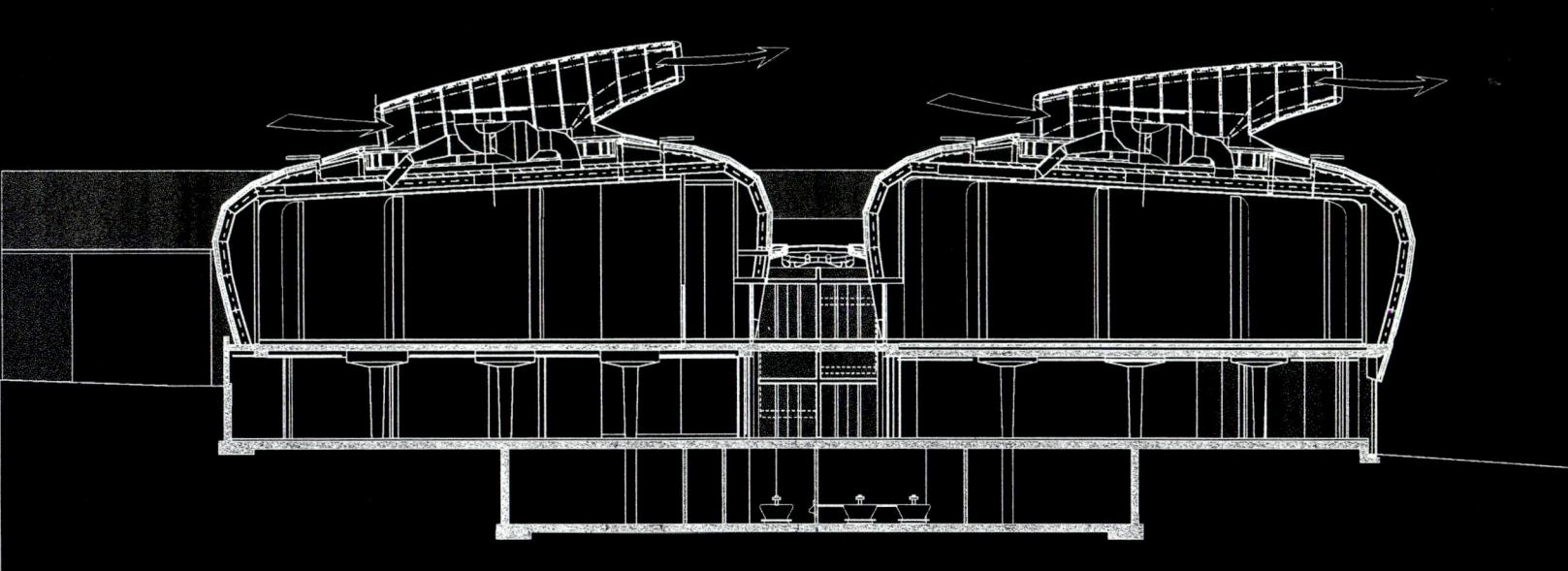

Section

FROM ABOVE: Rendering of interior and exterior view

FOREIGN OFFICE ARCHITECTS
VIRTUAL HOUSE: POTENTIAL BEYOND THE FUTURE

Traditionally, innovative and visionary architectures have been associated with the invention of the future. However, FOA is not interested in the future, but in the virtual, as a source of new architectural possibilities. The idea of the future implies an expressed recognition of the discontinuity of time into fixed frames, as if the process of actualisation of a certain reality were independent of a continuous process of change. FOA sees the future, the past, the present as static, believing that only the virtual is able to capture the dynamic nature of a situation or organisation by extending the real towards the potentials and the memories that it contains.

The Virtual House was commissioned by Any Corporation/FSB Brackel in 1997 in order to explore the idea of the virtual in a domestic project. It researched a form of habitation in order to unfold potentials beyond the given identities of form, function and place. But it is impossible to produce the virtual unless it is seen as a changing system of relationships, triggered by a certain process. The virtual will always move systematically out of one's grasp just as it becomes actualised. It is not possible to produce the virtual itself, only its potential actualisations, or a process that will trigger them.

FOA's attempt in this project was to unfold the effects that a physical structural system would produce in the given identities and forms of the dwelling. Its strategy to produce the virtual was not to replace the real with a sophisticated surrogate, as in 'virtual reality', but rather to dismantle the complex assemblage of social uses, organisations of space and material qualities that have come to constitute what we generally understand as a house. The architects believe that the virtual is not the better, the future or the past, but what may unfold or inherit a series of lineages.

In this search for potentials, FOA

focused first on the ground. The Virtual House would not become a figure imposed onto the ground, but would construct it. This virtual ground would not be an abstract and generic platform, a pedestal, but rather, concrete and specific. This virtual groundlessness would not have the verticality of the *Poeme de L'Angle Droit*, for it would no longer be in dimensional opposition to the ground. The construction of the Virtual House would no longer be an act of domination over matter and nature, but rather the act by which an artificial nature is produced, as an extension of singularities rather than as a field of resemblance.

The project emerged from a piece of artificial matter with indeterminate structural strength in terms of compression and tension, supplied with water and energy, and characterised phenomenally as a visually differentiated field. This field of visual singularity was made using Disruptive Pattern Material. DPM is produced by abstracting a given visual field into a differentiated distribution of colour on the surface of an object. It is specific not only in terms of its relation to a given visual field, but also in terms of its scale, dependent on the distance at which it is perceived.

FOA's new matter provided its Virtual House with a broad palette of abstracted regions, a collection of synthetic landscapes. The architects could now explore the groundlessness of the house by producing different models of ground, to proliferate the house into a series: the Arizona model, the Kwai model, the Steppe model, the Schwarzwald model and so forth.

This band of synthetic ground could be manipulated to produce the coding of space in a similar form in which a protein band folds to produce a DNA code: the organisation of matter would have precedence over the coding. It was manipulated in order to further challenge other

categories that have been characteristic of the domestic spatial phenomenology, such as the opposition between inside/outside, front/back, up/down, and other cultural constructions of the dwelling.

In order to challenge the conventional categories of inhabitation, each face of the folded DPM surface would shift from a lining condition to a wrapping condition, disrupting the orientation of the relationships between the enveloping surface and the inside/outside opposition. Interior spaces would be generated by topological handles in the surface band. Each room would then combine with another to form a double-sided, double-used band. Each composite band would be combined with other composite bands to produce a more complex organisation of rooms, in which the folding bands would also grow three-dimensionally, as a pile of wafer matter. The rooms would not be segmented parts of the structure, but, conversely, singular points in a continuous space.

In order to explore the gradients of different conditions occurring on the folded surface, preceding the coding of inhabitation, the different areas were classified into three possible qualities of surface: wrapping/lining, inside/outside, and gravity in/gravity out. The superposition of the gradients of these three different categorisations would produce the instructions for the use of this topography of inhabitation. The distribution of supplies from the surface would be made not in respect to functional spaces, but as an overall act dependent on the specificity of the topography.

The system could now proliferate the body of the house *ad infinitum*, like a deep, inhabited, hollow ground, from the room to the city. Or it could perhaps deform itself into variations of the basic room. The Virtual House is not an organic, finished body, but a proliferating structure where the rooms are not functionally determined, and yet are specific.

FROM ABOVE: Front elevation; Collection of landscapes; Elevation

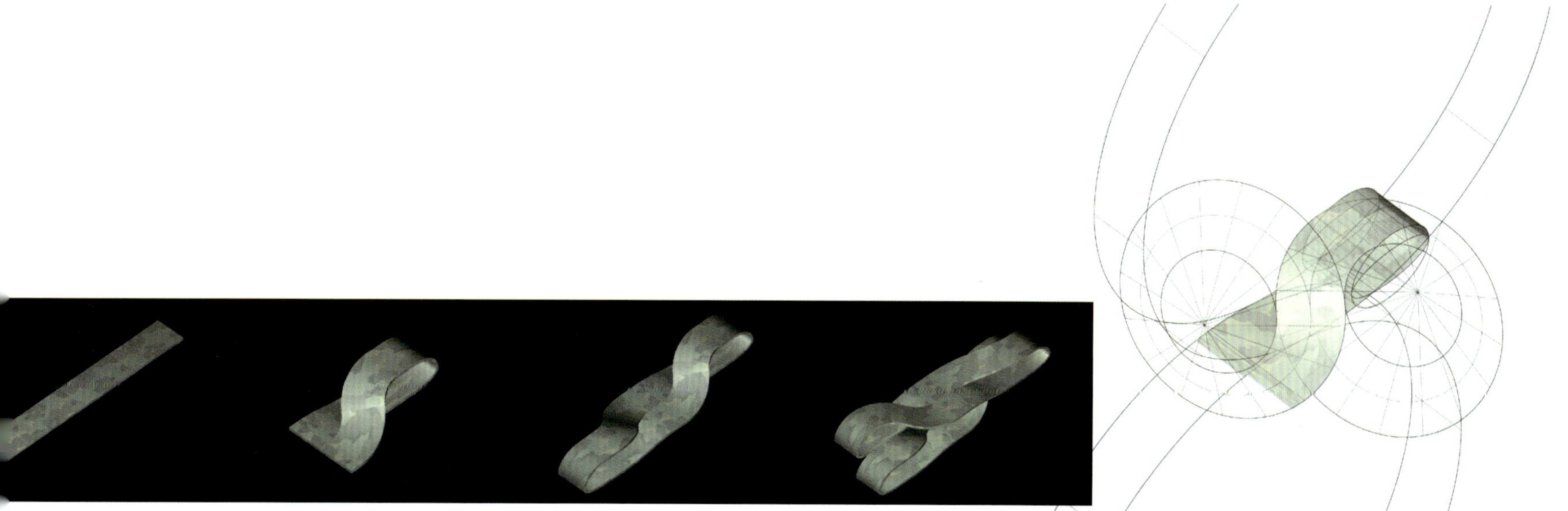

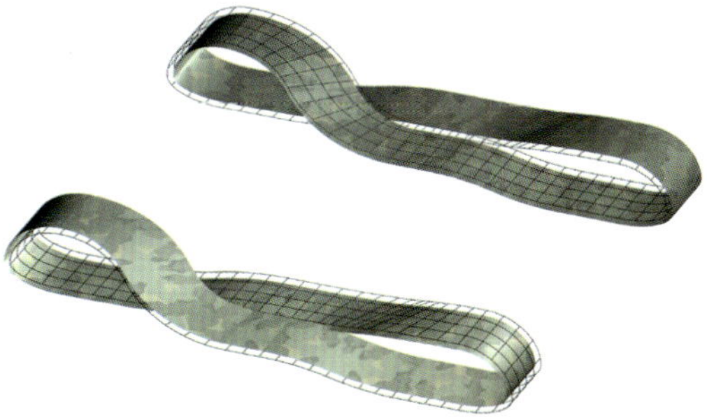

*FROM ABOVE: Side elevation; Sections;
Collection of landscapes; Image diagrams*

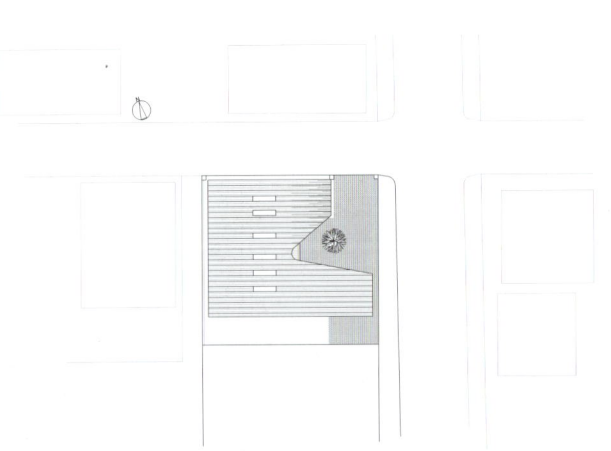

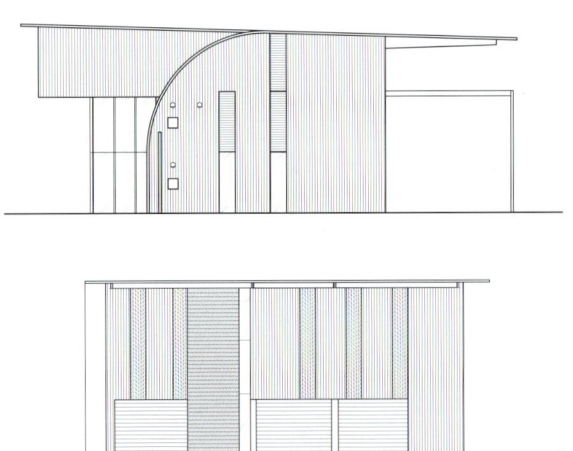

SHUHEI ENDO
FACILITY FOR A PARK
Hyogo Prefecture, Japan

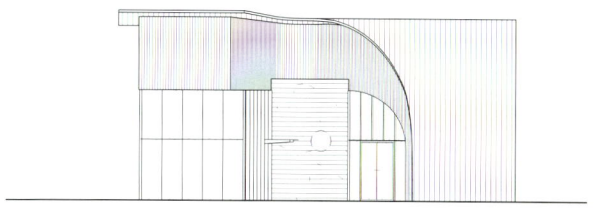

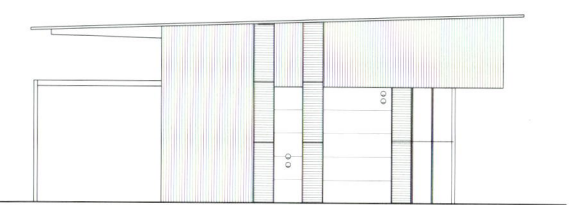

This public convenience for a small park is sited in a highly artificial location in the mountains of Hyogo Prefecture, Japan. As a facility for general use, of a kind that can be found anywhere in Japan, it defies any expression of regional character. Sandwiched by newly built elementary and secondary-school buildings, it has a simple structure comprising three sections: a janitor's room, and men's and women's lavatories.

Apparently a simple assemblage of parts, it is described as 'Halftecture', since it is characterised simultaneously by the open and the closed. Openness is provided by the possibility of passage in three directions, with no clearly defined entrance. This avoids the defensiveness that is created, paradoxically, by demarcated openings and the transparency of glass.

The whole facility is a structure for passage, suggesting the possibility of entrance from almost anywhere. At the same time, closedness as a spatial attribute is achieved by the use of an independent spiral of corrugated steel sheet roofs, walls and floors, with gate-shaped auxiliary materials partially inserted, to which permeability is added by the 3.2-millimetre clearance of reversed steel sheets.

OPPOSITE: Site plan; north and west elevations;
ABOVE: East and south elevations

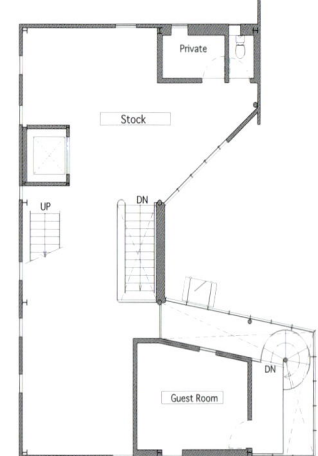

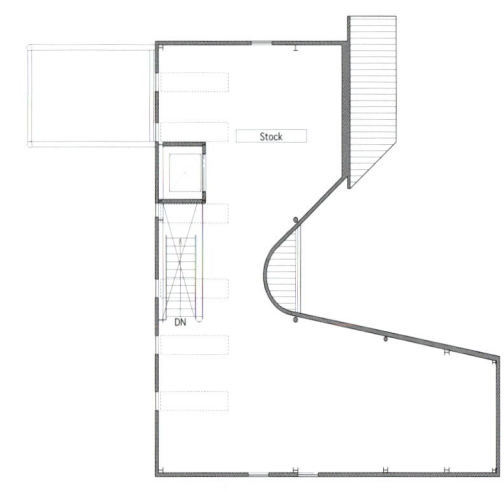

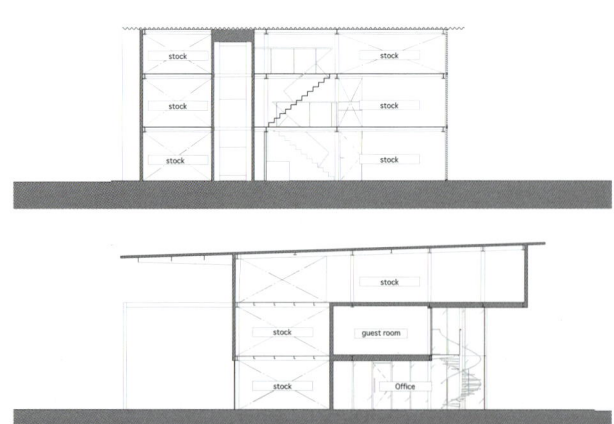

SHUHEI ENDO
ROOFTECTURE
Hyogo Prefecture, Japan

This building comprises an office and a three-floor temporary storage area for building materials. It is located at the corner of a busy intersection. A curved metal wall, merging with the roof, reduces the sense of oppression from the corner and uses the limited space as effectively as possible. The aim was to break away from the usual idea of an architecture formed by structure, towards a new concept of an architecture in which each building forms itself.

In ground plan, the building is C-shaped. The office is glazed on its south-eastern face, overlooking a tree in the centre of the area. On the second floor is a small, closed conference room. The expansive storage space is on three floors to the west of the building,

with high exterior eaves to facilitate the delivery of materials. The stairs are positioned at different points on each floor.

A wooden loading shaft goes through two floors, which are made of a light-permeable expanded metal to enhance strength, sound, natural light and ventilation, and to give a feeling of fluid clarity. Entering through a rectangular skylight on the roof and via long windows in the wall, belts of light permeate the first floor through the second and third. This gives the three-floor space the appearance of a one-floor room.

The exterior wall is covered with the same thin metal plate of silver and black, except for the front, which is of Japanese cedar.

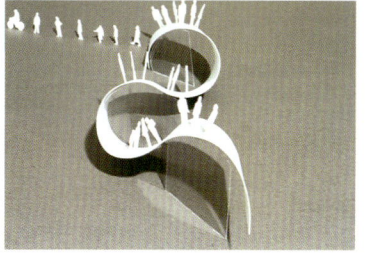

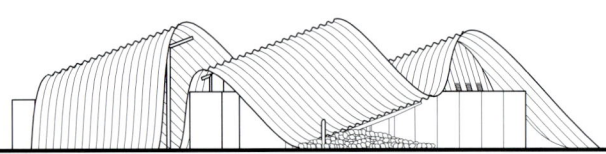

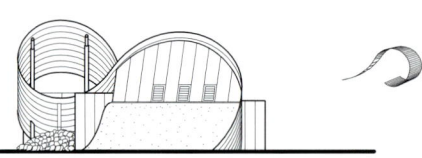

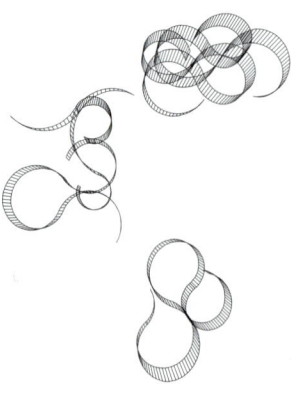

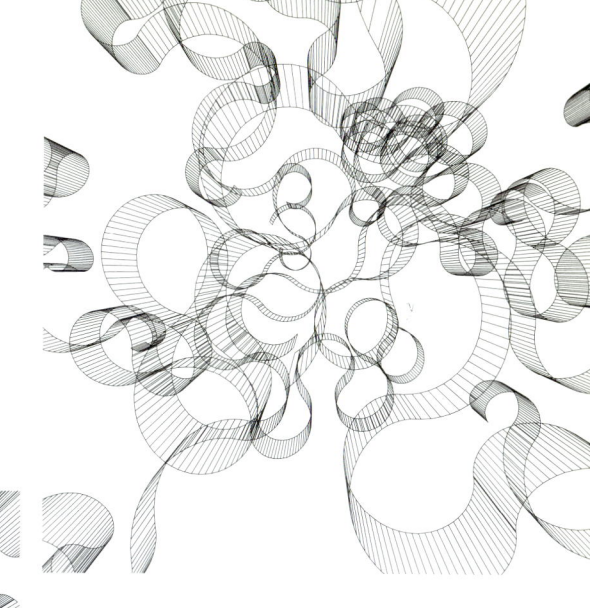

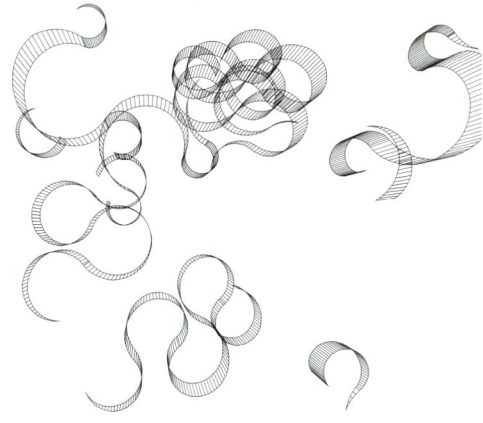

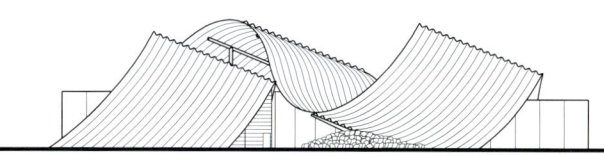

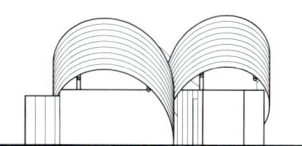

OPPOSITE L to R: East elevation; north elevation; FROM ABOVE L to R: Conceptual multiplication; west elevation; south elevation

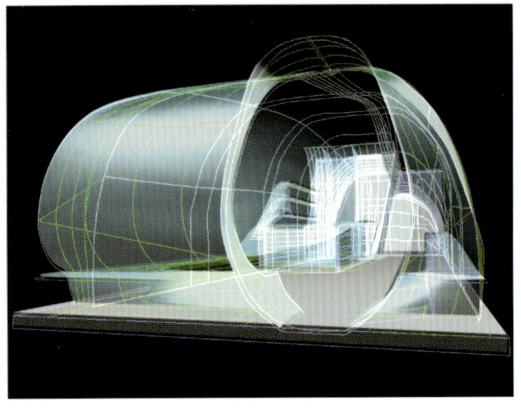 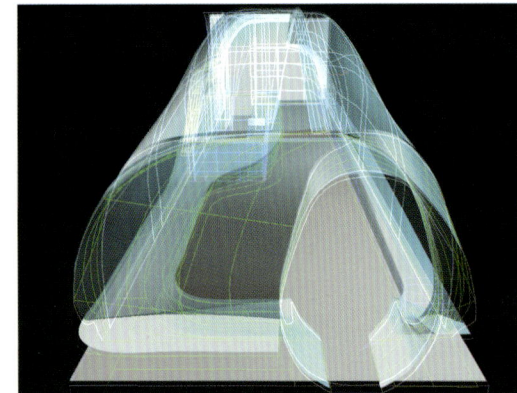 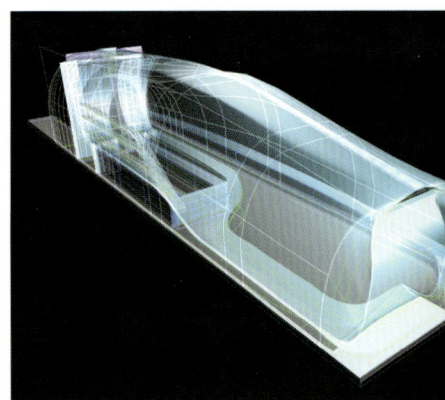

Glow Bar, Melbourne, Australia, 1998
ABOVE: Entry detail; CENTRE: Front
perspective; RIGHT AND BELOW:
External/ internal surface relationship

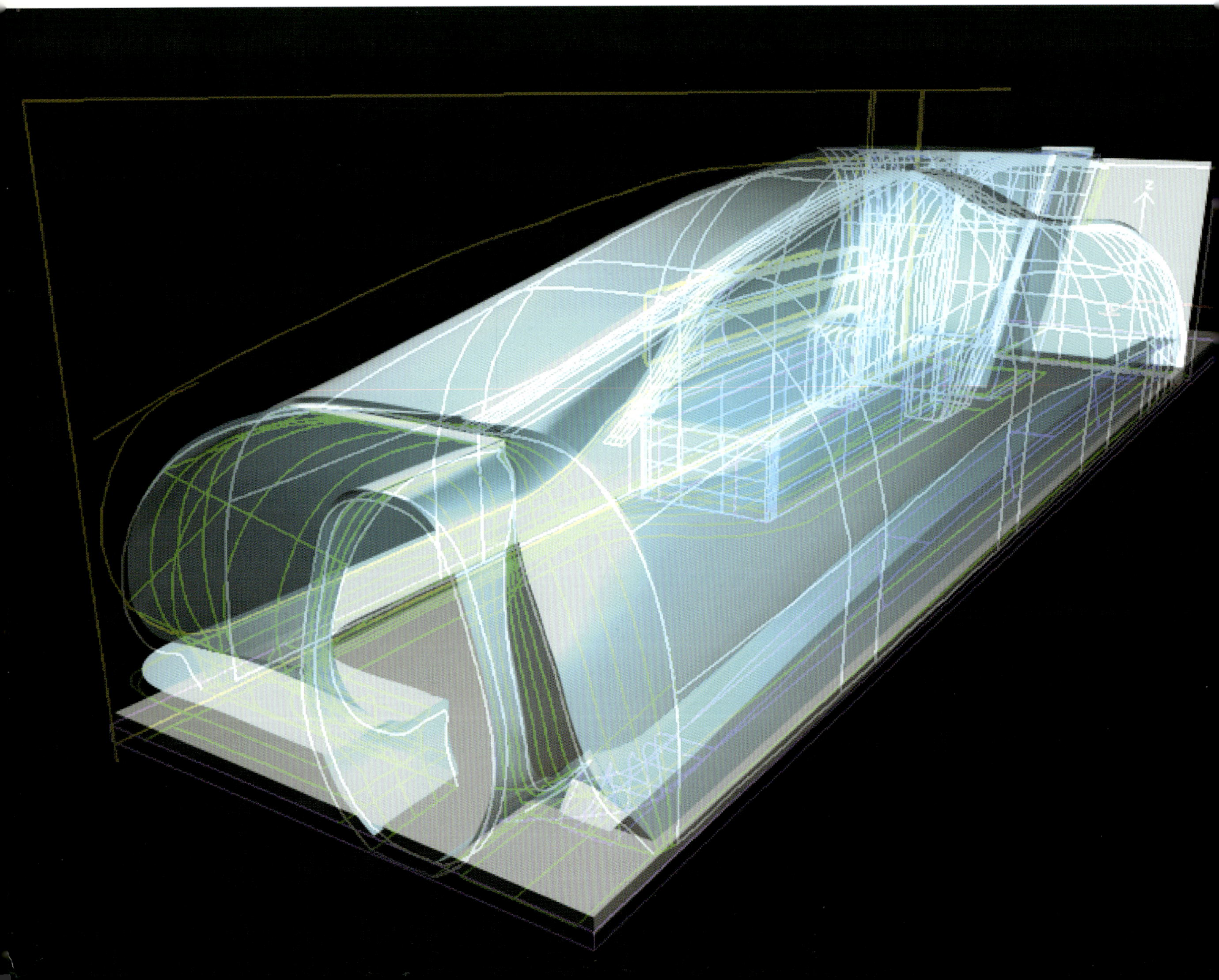

KOVAC MALONE

SCIENCE-FICTION ARCHITECTURE

Leon van Schaik

Singapore always strikes me as an improbable place. Self-made, self-willed, it seems to me to defy reality. The dream that has given it shape is still so vividly present that I feel I'm living in a novel, or that I'm a bit-part player in a film – a little anonymous and reduced, like an inhabitant of Alphaville. I stay in the Westin Stamford, 'the world's tallest hotel'. Recently, I discovered that this complex reflects your desires back at you in utterly unexpected ways. I used to think that all I had to fear was the incremental vertigo afforded by location on the 16th, 28th, 43rd, or 59th floor. But in the diurnal tide of humanity through this super-block, more is divined and reflected back. It is as paralysingly attractive and utterly empty as its heartlessly casual design style.

I am reminded of an episode in the BBC series *Journey into Space* in which the characters are willed into an Australian Outback scene through the mental jujitsu of their Martian pursuers. Science fiction is necessarily a projection of our desires, just as cities are layers of such projections mouldering on top of one another (Rowe's Collage City), or rubbing harshly against each other (Shane's Collision City). But science fiction is narrower: it is the projection of futures dreamed up by a solo vision. Singapore is so new that the edges of the vision show up starkly, and in its seamless cleanliness you discover you can drop through desire into horror.

Into this reverie crackles the voice of Geoff Malone, Singapore-based partner in Kovac Malone Architecture: 'Leon, let's have lunch. The Tiffin Room at Raffles for a change. See you in the foyer in an hour'. I tear myself away from the djinns of an evil future, and an hour later we walk into a make-believe room of the Raj. Over the Mulligatawny soup – a science-fiction concoction if ever there was one – he looks at me quizzically and asks: 'What do your students make of Nano-technology?'

Now, I'm a little prepared for this. I've sat through official dinners at which physicists have spoken in awed tones about these microscopic, molecular scale engines that will replace the machines of our world with an invisibly knitted Utopia in which veins can be repaired by marshalling cells and setting them to work. And I've spent some hours in Tom Kovac's 'Streamline' studio trying to understand how carbon-fibre

filaments, laced exactly through stress patterns, are going to bring into being the Little La Trobe Street Apartments – a 15-storey block towering above four-storey buildings inside what the State Government planners now call 'the RMIT innovation precinct'. I've seen the beginnings of this project, and been asked to endorse it on behalf of RMIT. Its 'part walls' are contoured like muscles to the stress patterns of the construction, and the long shape is as smooth as an 18th-century tortoise-shell spectacle case. I've seen how different arrangements of molecules can construct a completely impervious, all-in-one surface that changes from solid and massive to thin and transparent without any junctions at all. It's just matter variously organised to meet different specifications for thermal performance, viewing cones, rates of flow of queues, atmosphere and so forth.

'Not much', I respond, 'and it's a pity, because we're casting about for ways to enliven their concern for this now that CAD seems to make anything that it is possible to describe buildable'. In a flash, I'm part of that glint in Geoff's eye.

The Tiffin Room, which has brought into being a future based on a version of the past that outdoes that past for novelistic authenticity, is an apt location for a series of rethinks about Kovac's approach. In previous writings on the construction of his spatial capsules, I've referred to an archaic image: armies of white-clad artisans smearing on layers of gesso. This image was brought about by seeing photographs of Kiesler's Bucephalus or Endless House/ Theatre models. But even if the extraordinary background webbing that holds some of Kovac's surfaces in place is reminiscent of the space on top of the dome of St Paul's Cathedral, and the effect outdoes in accuracy any of the surfaces in Scharoun's Philharmonic or Gehry's Guggenheim, it is the lines that he draws that predict the built future of his designs, and these lines have an uncanny accuracy.

Gaudí's lines had just such a connection to the lines of structural forces. Current mathematical modelling reveals how sophisticated this understanding was, just as powerfully as it fails to deal with the aesthetic that Gaudí created from his structural intuition. This is a pointer to the problem of description in science

Queen Street Bar, *Melbourne, Australia, 1998*
ABOVE: Bar/ shelving detail; BELOW: Internal perspective

fiction: leave out key elements and you project the same sort of appalling rubbish that is finding its way onto the Sagrada Familia. Kovac's design is more than a set of calculations. What is now working its way out in the Little La Trobe Street Apartment Building is a new vision.

Glow, a tiny space-capsule bar in Acland Street St Kilda, just round the corner from where I'm writing, is deeply layered into Melbourne's traditional bohemian holiday resort and mercifully distant from the so-far virtual temptations of Singapore. The Kovac Malone approach to this project was to computer-simulate it and then to prefabricate it off site without model or mock-up, 'like a Boeing 777', says Tom. Sitting in it as the light fades, the surfaces are slowly suffused with blue from a vertical panel at the rear; the street is drained of substance, becoming a set of flickering lights etched onto the plate-glass stopper of the tube, and I realise that this approach was possible because of the lines that delineate the design.

Nano-technology has inspired Kovac Malone to down-load an image of the future into a set of programmed molecules that first grow a swarm of helpers and then herd together other molecules to form over a period of time (as long in duration as conventional construction or longer?) a self-repairing capsule. This ranges from gilled white opaque matter, to blue translucent matter, to clear transparent matter, to something that completely resembles say, travertine – *is* travertine – cannot be molecularly told apart from travertine – as long as the designer's description is good enough.

Here I pause to reflect on my concern that Kovac's surface should find some expression more appropriate to its shimmering presence than matte-white-painted gypsum board – perhaps a Tom Kovac version of Yves Klein International Blue that would stand for the lines of the fast drawings that bring his spaces into being. Maybe now there could be capsules that

are Nano-formed into seamless alabaster, self supporting, self colouring . . . Kovac International Stuff? It reeks of the future.

Back to the 'Streamline' studio. This is another bit of the past's future, firmly lodged in the present, but speaking exclusively of the 1950s dream that created it. Inside a radiator-grille-like corner wedge is the office; below, there is the Queen Street Bar. Into the floor plan, shaped like an arrow head, Kovac cut an arc across the rhomboid of the building footprint, dividing the space into a service zone and a bar in the corner wedge. The ceilings and walls are gilled in an internal reflection of the decorative *brise soleil* above. Light, in the familiar Kovac manner, is used to modulate the space.

More like the endless ante-rooms of intergalactic ships lost in space is the Hyper-centre: a series of people-management space prototypes that can be hooked onto a range of entertainment facilities anywhere, ensuring a corporate identity and a uniform standard of service wherever they're installed. Of course, we've seen these capsules before, but usually on the scale of bathrooms. These Hyper-centres bring weightlessness to the waiting rooms of the world. I hope their efficiency transcends the anomie that seems to result in the suppressed aggression that roils through the space ships of science fiction.

In a recent documentary about life in the universe a sociologist observed that while there might well be life on planets in other galaxies, the ambition of scientists to build space-ship colonies that would eventually reach the inhabited planets might be thwarted by the fact that space travellers would be so consumed by faction fighting and ethnic cleansing that the ship would be classified DOA: Dead On Arrival. I get a whiff of that stupefaction in some of these whirling chambers, but then, I suffer from claustrophobia. Most club-goers do not. What these spaces do offer that is ahead of the sci-fi

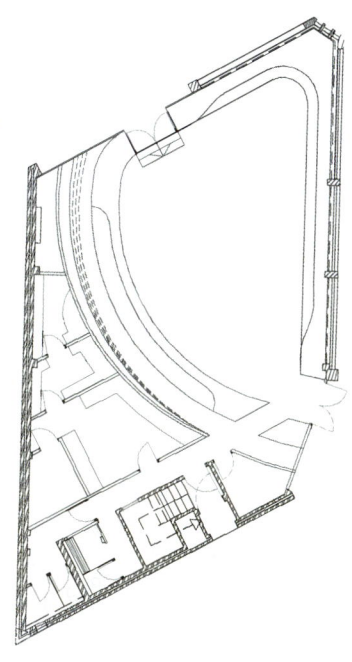

Queen Street Bar, Melbourne, Australia, 1998
ABOVE: Floor plan; BELOW L TO R: South elevation; west elevation; side entry

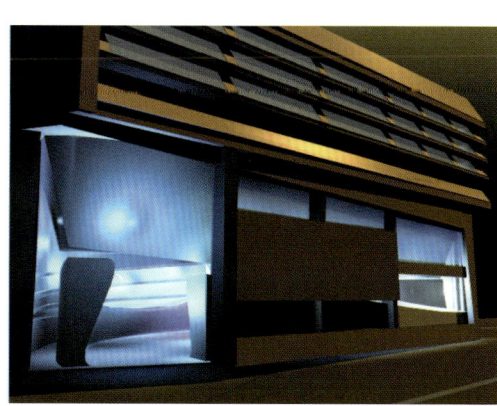
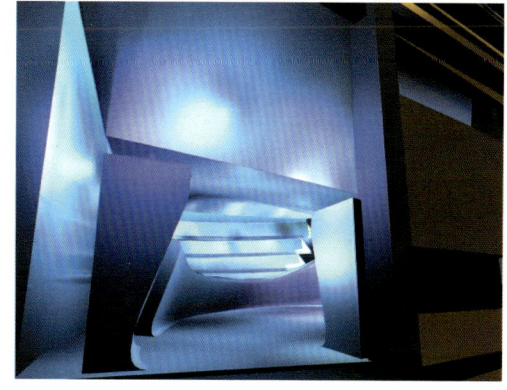

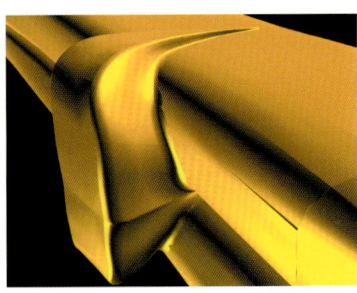

Hypercentre, Europe, 1998
ABOVE: Corridor, internal
perspective and external shell;
BELOW: External perspective of
foyer detail; RIGHT: Circulation

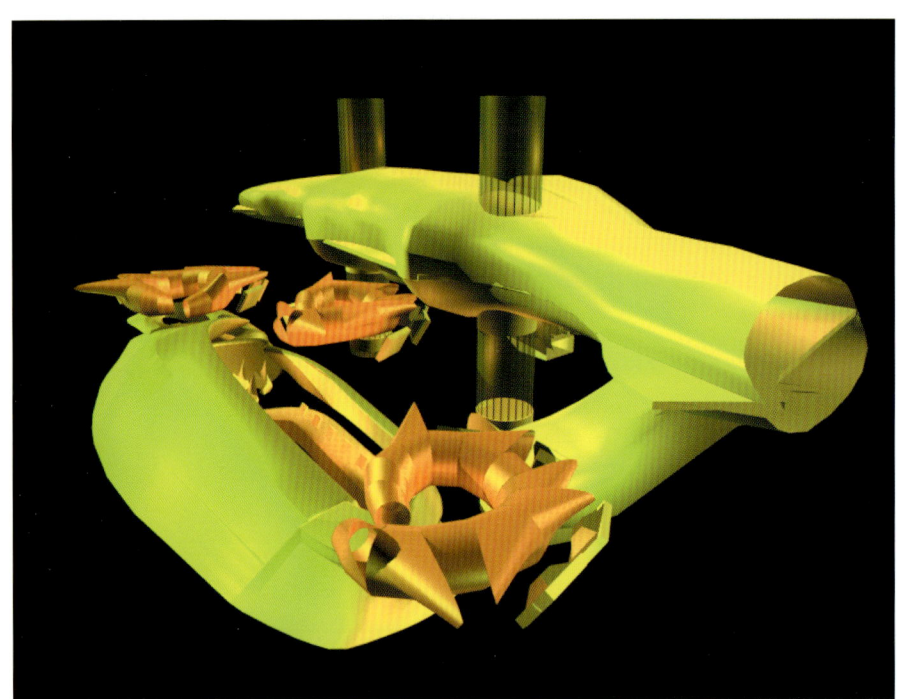

movies and in accord with developing glass technologies – as Michael Trudgeon's 1998 Seppelt Environmental Design Award Hyperhouse demonstrates – is a continuous, live, combined wall/ceiling surface that changes endlessly, supersaturated not with colour or material but with super-graphic information.

As a southerner, born in colonial dominion, I have been haunted by one particular science-fiction tale ever since I read it as a boy. It seems to me to capture the projective ambition that is the best effect of displacement or diaspora. In this tale, a space ship is stranded on an unknown planet, all technological capability destroyed in a crash landing. What does survive is the *Encyclopedia Britannica*. From this, over some generations, the survivors construct a civilisation. When a ship from the Old World eventually happens on this community, its captain is aghast to find that the culture that has been created from literal interpretations of the glowing descriptions in the encyclopedia far exceeds the original in achievement. Visionary architects are very like these unintentional colonials: dreaming up descriptions of possible futures and pushing the technology of their times towards describable, but as yet unseen, unverifiable outcomes.

There is one Kovac Malone image that captures this for me, even more than most. The Little La Trobe Street Apartment Building is shown against a red, rocket-spattered, millennial sky. The structural web of carbon-fibre cords is etched in white light, and the surfaces are all either transparent or translucent. The angled balconies, however, reflect light back at the sunbursts in the night sky. At its foot, the humdrum orthogonals of the existing Corrigan and Neometro urban fabric are dark or picked

out in the green afterglow of the flash. An image from *Bladerunner* replaces its Kurosawa opposite. Aside from the extraordinarily sculptural sinuosity of the building itself, what am I seeing? It seems that the fibre of the structure is doubling up as an optic-cable information system that is also a light source. It is this simultaneity that the work strains towards: a technology far in advance of the aluminium-cable trays of the Boeing, and infinitely removed from the re-styling of the neo-classical into a machined aesthetic of reduction by that great pamphleteer of A-New-World-To-Come: Le Corbusier.

I am, however, also haunted by another, less reassuring science-fiction story of the 1960s. This tale suggests that the whole of the evolution of consciousness on earth is a device set in train by a civilisation light years away, which is trying to rescue its stranded time-travellers. Lacking the technical capability or ability to communicate on Earth, they require a small plastic bar with a slot in it to return to their planet.

The entire history of our culture, our music and our cathedrals, is all evolved in a series of fits and starts in order to get us to manufacture these spare parts. Finally, the emergence of the consumer culture produces the disposable sticks for ice lollies that are exactly what is needed. The space travellers retrieve one and are on their way, leaving us to our own, or more properly, as our own devices.

We do indeed hover on the edge of hubris when we are visionary. It could go either way: we could end up living more switched on to our cities and our communities; or we could enter into a placelessness that even Marc Auge of Non Places could not imagine.

Little Latrobe Street, Melbourne, Australia, 1998 ABOVE: North West elevation; BELOW: South perspective

BIOGRAPHIES

RACHEL ARMSTRONG is a television presenter for new technology on BBC's *UK Arena* and for Sky Television. She is also a multimedia producer, medical doctor, and writer specialising in the evolution of humankind. She is currently working on her new book, *A Gray's Anatomy.*

BRANSON COATES ARCHITECTS was set up by Doug Branson and Nigel Coates in London, 1985. Branson studied and taught architecture at Canterbury College of Art and Architecture, and the Architectural Association in London, where Coates also taught from 1976-86. In 1995, Coates was appointed Professor of Architectural Design at the Royal College of Art. The team has a strong reputation for innovative design. Recent projects include the extension to the Geffrye Museum in London. Currently, they are architectural designers for the Millennium Dome's Body Zone.

COOP HIMMELB(L)AU is headed by architects Wolf Prix and Helmut Swiczinsky, producing work notable for its deconstruction of form, evident in the Rooftop Remodelling, Vienna, 1983-89. Among their many projects are the Biennale Pavillion, Venice, 1995 and the recent UFA – Cinema Centre in Dresden, 1994-97.

KARIN DAMRAU graduated in 1995 from FHT, Stuttgart, later studying in Bordeaux and Zurich. She then worked as an architect in Hamburg for two years before receiving a grant from the German Academic Exchange Service to study for a Master's degree at the Bartlett School of Architecture, University College London, from which she graduated with distinction in 1998.

SHUHEI ENDO obtained a master's degree at Kyoto University of Art in 1986 and two years later established the Shuhei Endo Architect Institute. He is a lecturer at Kobe Design University and has produced many award-winning projects. Recent work includes Transtation O, 1997, and Springtecture H, 1998.

FIN ARCHITECTS AND DESIGNERS (Future is now) was established by Andy Martin in 1996, who originates from Australia and studied architecture at the Institute of Technology, NSW and the Architectural Association in London. In 1989 he returned to Australia, establishing a small practice that concentrated mainly on domestic architecture and furniture. On his return to Europe in 1991, he made a base in Paris, expanding to London in 1997. He continues to works on restaurants, residential and hotel projects.

FOREIGN OFFICE ARCHITECTS was founded in 1993 to explore contemporary production processes as sources of new architectural possibilities. In 1995, it was awarded first prize in the Yokohama International Port Terminal Competition. Since then, it has been involved in speculative projects and competitions for large-scale urban operations: transport systems, public spaces and leisure. Directors Farshid Moussavi and Alejandro Zaera-Poloby hold positions at the Architectural Association, Columbia University, the Berlage Institut and Princeton University.

FTL is an architecture/engineering practice formed in the USA by Todd Dalland and Nicholas Goldsmith. It specialises in the design and construction of innovative buildings using tensile membranes. The practice has designed many major projects across the Eastern seaboard of the USA and was one of the major designers of the 1996 Atlanta Olympic Games.

KOLATAN/MACDONALD STUDIO was founded in 1986 by Sulan Kolatan and William J MacDonald. The firm has received many awards and its work is in the permanent collections of the Museum of Modern Art, New York, San Francisco Museum of Modern Art, and the Avery Library Collection. Recent exhibitions were held at the Deutsches Architektur Museum, Frankfurt, Columbia University and the Sandra Gering Gallery, New York.

KOVAC MALONE was founded in 1997 by Tom Kovac and Geoffrey Malone. Born in Slovenia, Kovac currently resides in Melbourne where the practice has built many adventurous residential buildings, bars and restaurants. He studied architecture at RMIT University, Australia, and is now a tutor in Design there. He established Kovac Architecture in 1990, and in 1994, set up the Curve Architecture Gallery, Melbourne. Currently, Kovac Malone is creating an large screen cinema in Singapore.

REISER + UMEMOTO comprises Jesse Reiser, fellow of the American Academy in Rome and adjunct assistant professor of architecture at Columbia University, and Nanako Umemoto, formerly adjunct assistant professor of urban design at Osaka University of Art and now assistant professor of architecture at Columbia University.

SCHNEIDER & SCHUMACHER studied architecture together in Kaiserlautern, Germany. Both went on to postgraduate studies at the Städelschule in Frankfurt, under Peter Cook. Later, Til Schneider worked for Eisele + Fritz, while Michael Schumacher worked in London with Norman Foster and in Frankfurt with Branun and Schockermann. They became partners in 1989, practising in Frankfurt. Their work is characterised by its adventurous use of light.

TAKASAKI MASAHARU began as an artist and sculptor. After graduating from Meijo University, he worked with professors at Stuttgart University and the Graz Institute of Technology. He founded Mono-Bito Institute in Tokyo in 1982 and Takasaki Masaharu Architects in Kagoshima in 1990. His spiritually conceived work has won numerous awards.

BERNARD TSCHUMI is based in New York and Paris. He studied in Paris and at the Federal Institute of Technology (ETH), Zurich and has taught at the Architectural Association in London, the Institute for Architecture and Urban Studies in New York, Princeton University, and Cooper Union, USA. He is currently Chief Architect of the Parc de la Villette and Dean of the Graduate School of Architecture, Planning and Preservation at Columbia University, New York. He is a member of the College International de Philosophie, and was awarded the Grand Prix National d'Architecture in 1996. Current projects include the Ecole d'Architecture, Marne la Vallée, France.

VAN BERKEL & BOS was set up by Ben Van Berkel and Caroline Bos in Amsterdam, 1988. Projects included industrial schemes such as the Karbouw an ACOM office buildings and the REMU electricity station; several housing projects, and the interior of the Aedes East gallery, Berlin. Recent work includes a new museum for Nijmegen and a museum extension in Enschede, various housing and mixed-use projects, and the Erasmus Bridge in Rotterdam. Van Berkel was visiting professor at Columbia University in New York, and Diploma Unit Master at the Architectural Association in London, from which he graduated in 1987.

LEO VAN SCHAIK is Dean of the Faculty of the Constructed Environment and Professor of Architecture at the Royal Melbourne Institute of Technology.